PAPA'S PLACE

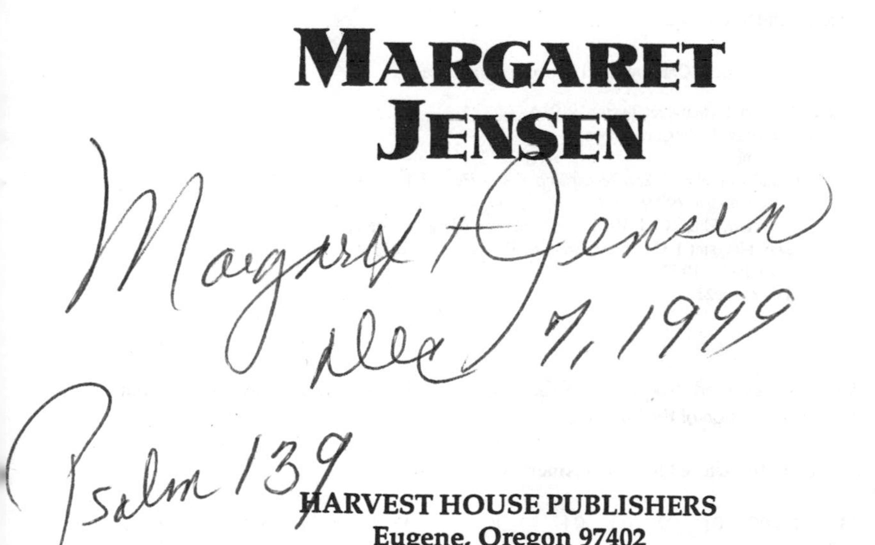

MARGARET JENSEN

HARVEST HOUSE PUBLISHERS
Eugene, Oregon 97402

Scripture quotations are taken from the King James Version of the Bible.

Cover by Left Coast Design, Portland, Oregon.

PAPA'S PLACE

Published by Harvest House Publishers
Eugene, Oregon 97402

Library of Congress Cataloging-in-Publication Data

Jensen, Margaret T. (Margaret Tweten), 1916–
Papa's place / Margaret Jensen.
p. cm.
Originally published: San Bernardino, CA : Here's Life Publishers, © 1987.
ISBN 1-56507-798-9
1. Tweten, Elius N., d. 1973. 2. Baptists—Clergy—Biography.
3. Jensen, Margaret T. (Margaret Tweten), 1916– . I. Title.
BX6495.T8J46 1998
286'.1'092—dc21
[B] 97-29019
CIP

Printed in the United States of America.

98 99 00 01 02 03 04 / BC / 10 9 8 7 6 5 4 3 2 1

Dedicated to Papa's children

The Grandchildren

Margaret's Children:
Janice Jensen Carlberg
Daniel Jensen
Ralph Jensen

Gordon's Children:
Ray Tweten
Nancy Tweten Fjordbatten
Don Tweten
Kurt Tweten

Doris' Children:
Doreen Hammer Mabe
Donald Hammer
Davidson Hammer
Duane Hammer

Joyce Solveig's Children:
Judy Jensen Marschewski
Paul Jensen
Steve Jensen

Jeanelle's Children:
Robert Keiter
Charlene Keiter Strand

Contents

Sing, O heavens;
and be joyful, O earth;
and break forth into singing, O mountains:
for the Lord hath comforted his people,
and will have mercy upon his afflicted.

—Isaiah 49:13

And when ye stand praying,
forgive, if ye have ought against any:
that your Father also
which is in heaven
may forgive you your trespasses.

—Mark 11:25

Special Thanks

A special thanks to Harvest House for getting *Papa's Place* back into circulation.

I thank my sisters who learned with me to build a bridge of understanding over our troubled waters.

I thank my readers—friends—across the miles who are encouraged to bring love and understanding through their stormy seas.

I thank God that His way is perfect and His love never fails. The mystery is that He sends us, the imperfect ones, with that message of hope into the marketplace.

Introduction

The Episcopal rector and I sat together watching the people fill the fellowship hall for a church banquet.

Tonight I would be sharing stories from my book *First We Have Coffee,* a book about Mama and her coffeepot—but more than that, a book about God's faithfulness through a special child of His. Laughter and tears flow through the pages.

"I loved your book, Margaret," the priest whispered to me, "but your mother was an angel." He shrugged offhandedly. "Who can identify with her? Why don't you write about Papa? He sounds like quite a character—and someone with whom we mortals can relate."

We laughed together, then the meeting began.

Some months later my daughter, Janice, suggested the title "Papa's Place." Papa called Janice his "princess," and she loved him.

Still I hesitated.

Did I really want to tell Papa's story? I wanted my children and my grandchildren to know that Papa was a godly man. But did I want them to know that this strong, sturdy Norwegian, who had been loved by so many, was given to anger and could explode easily? Even more, did I want to admit the pain, the hurt that I often had felt as a child, or that at times I actually had feared my father?

Did I want to portray both sides of my beloved Papa, to tarnish his pastoral image with my own raw memories of his one prevailing flaw? I looked at my daughter, Janice, and then across the room to her children, my grandchildren.

Yes, my children and my grandchildren had a right to know Papa Tweten as he was, the fallible, flesh-and-blood man I knew and loved. He was part of their roots—the branch from which they sprang. There was joy in telling Mama's story—she was so loving, so caring, so full of faith. But both Mama and Papa were part of my children's heritage.

Mama and Papa! Mama was like a flowing river, blessing the banks of life around her. Papa was like a mountain stream rushing through rocks and brush to reach the river. He knew his source—God. But he found his rightful place when the restless stream met the river—Mama.

Now I was going back to a long-ago time. I was remembering Papa . . .

1

The Journey

Mama packed a box with clean clothes, carefully folded, so as not to wrinkle my starched dresses and petticoats. Two were for everyday; one was for Sunday. Papa's white shirt lay on top. Then she closed up the box, and I followed her outside where Papa was cranking up the old Model-T Ford with its thin tires and snap-on curtains. With a quick smile he kissed Mama, Grace, Gordon, and Doris goodbye. As Mama held me tightly, the lump in my throat grew bigger. My younger sisters and brother lined up to kiss me and stood in awe of this astonishing occasion.

I was going with Papa on a missionary journey!

We were leaving our home at 510 Avenue J, Saskatoon, Saskatchewan, to drive on the open roads through the Canadian prairie. As we pulled away that bright summer day in 1928, I waved until the four-room, white-trimmed yellow house with the outhouse in back faded into the distance. In my mind I could see Mama putting on the coffeepot and the children dipping their sugar lumps into Mama's coffee.

Papa and I drove over the dusty roads in silence. Communicating with his children was not Papa's place. It was up to God and Mama to bring up Mama's children. He had the

Lord's work to do. Papa taught theology; Mama taught the living.

I didn't need to talk. It was enough to know that Papa told Mama he needed me. Papa wanted me along? This was history in the making! I didn't think he needed anyone, but I heard him tell Mama just before driving away, "The journey is long and Margaret is good company. Besides, she can play the organ in the tent meetings."

As the old black Ford rattled over the ruts in the road, I sat prim and proper with my hands folded in my lap—a scrawny twelve-year-old with bobbed blond hair and blue eyes almost as bright and clear as Papa's. A plain, full skirt stretched over my starched petticoat, partially hiding my gangly legs.

Unaware of me, Papa sang the old hymns in his clear tenor and practiced his Norwegian sermons in English since he preached in both languages.

I clutched my clean handkerchief and sat up straight. This was a moment to remember. Once or twice I stole a glance his way. I was in awe of my handsome father in his black suit and high starched collar. Papa was a clean-shaven man with a full face and high forehead and bushy blond eyebrows that overshadowed his piercing blue eyes. He was slender, barely six feet on tiptoe, but to me he was tall, a tower of strength.

I tried to remember Mama's instructions. "Keep Papa's clothes clean and be sure he has the starched white shirt for Sunday meeting." Mama had hugged me again and whispered, "I'll miss you, Margaret, and I'll miss you helping with the children." The lump in my throat came back.

From the open window of the car I watched the rolling fields of Saskatchewan and the isolated farmlands of the Norwegian immigrants. Towering pines stretched toward the sky. White clouds floated lazily in the blue expanse above us. The wind on the prairie sang a song of its own. But Papa was oblivious of me and of the splash of sun on the miles of grain waving in the summer wind. I relaxed, breathing deep—loving the earthen smell of wheat fields and barnyards.

When we came to the first farm, the children waved and the cattle stared at us with big brown eyes. Kittens and chickens scurried in the garden. The horses plodded along pulling the plow. They tugged at their restraints as the chugging, spouting Model-T roared down the lane, disrupting the quiet countryside.

The farmer's wife wiped her hands on her apron and offered us a drink of cold water or a cup of coffee. Papa and the farmer exchanged news and finally Papa extended an invitation to the tent meeting.

The children and I looked shyly at each other, then talked about kittens and things.

After a prayer for God's blessing on the farmer's family, Papa cranked up the Ford and we continued on our way.

"Ja, Margaret, we stay at the Thompson's house this time, and you will help Mrs. Thompson with the chores and housework. Deacon Salen's daughter Cora plays the organ at the tent meeting, but if she can't come, then you will play the hymns you have learned."

I promised to help Mrs. Thompson and play the organ. No one argued with Papa! We drifted back into silence. I was remembering another time on another farm—when I helped. I shuddered. That was the time Uncle Barney rescued Grace and me from our farm "vacation" where we scrubbed floors, rubbed clothes on a washboard, and ironed with irons heated on the wood stove. We weeded the garden, gathered eggs, and cleaned the separator after the milking. At night Grace and I crawled into bed, clinging to each other in utter despair and homesickness. We vowed never to leave Mama again!

This was different. Papa needed me! That was enough!

Mama was like a harbor, safe and secure, like a river deep and flowing. Papa was like a restless sea, with sudden flashes of temper like a summer storm. Then, just as suddenly, Papa's songs and laughter came back, like sunshine after rain. When the storms came we ran to Mama, who explained that Papa never understood children because he had never been a child.

Softly she would remind us, "Papa's parents died when he was very young. He never had a real childhood." She would hug us and add, "When he was seventeen years old he came to America to study." Perhaps Papa didn't understand children, but Mama said that he understood loneliness and fear.

It seemed that Mama understood everything—most of all Papa. She loved him.

The waving fields swept by while Papa sang old Norwegian songs. I was remembering another time, when I was six years old, a long time ago. It was the time Papa threw the rag doll, Big Jack, into the furnace.

I wept for my well-worn rag doll—my only one. But Papa thought it was part of the debris he swept up in the Winnipeg parsonage basement. Always in a hurry, he shoveled the contents into the furnace.

It was then that Mama explained, "Papa never had a toy and doesn't understand the ways of a rag doll and a six-year-old girl." She wiped my tears. "Besides, I will make a new rag doll for you. You must forgive Papa." I tried to forget about the rag doll, but I always remembered the little boy who didn't have a toy.

I stole another glance at Papa sitting up straight and tall, his broad hands on the steering wheel. He turned to me with a chuckle. "Ja, Margaret, so what do you think going with your Papa on a missionary journey—like Paul and Timothy?" He laughed with abandoned joy and sang "Standing on the Promises." He loved the freedom of the open road and his Model-T. And he loved the journey he was taking. This was Papa's parish—the scattered, Scandinavian immigrants of the province of Saskatchewan. The farmers lived miles apart, but that didn't bother Papa. "When I come they get together for meetings in the schoolhouse," he said, "or they pitch a tent in the summertime."

As though talking to himself he mused out loud, "The Scandinavian settlers are strong and full of faith. You'll see, Margaret. They learn to live with a new language, blizzards, even crop failures. But their greatest test is loneliness." His smile faded for a moment. "Some wait for years for their families to come from Europe. Some families never come. We are blessed, Margaret. We have Mama . . . there's no one like Mama." I turned. His blue eyes were on me. "The first time I saw your Mama I said, 'That is the wife for me!'" Papa chuckled delightedly. "I even forgot my sermon—but I married Mama three months later."

As we rode along, I forgot my awe of Papa and we talked about the time we came to Saskatchewan and lived in the chicken house. "Do you remember the chicken house, Papa?"

Papa's laughter rolled over the prairie as we remembered together. "The farmer? I see him now," Papa said. "I asked him for a house for my family to stay in."

"Ja, Ja," Papa said, mimicking the farmer. "Ve have a house for you for the summer. It vas our first home and I built it myself."

Behind the thorny bushes and scrub pine had stood a weather-beaten house hidden from view. When we reached it, I knew why it was hidden. Chickens flew in every direction cackling a loud protest over the eviction notice. Mice scampered, but not for long. Flies were everywhere. We peeked through the broken windows and walked on the loose floor boards. Spiderwebs clung to the walls. The doors squeaked on rusty hinges.

We laughed now as we bumped and bounced on the high, hard seats of the Model-T. But we didn't laugh back then. Papa continued, "Ja, I remember the farmer said, 'Plenty of food in the storehouse, and my vimmen vill see that you get vot you need. Come, I'll show you the storehouse before I go back to the fields.'"

The farmer's beautiful house stood on the hill, surrounded by gardens of flowers and vegetables. Across the road were barns and storehouses bursting with the fruits of plentiful harvests. Cattle and horses grazed in the lush pastures. Hired men worked in the fields. In the barn were buggies and wagons and a shiny new car.

I sighed. "I remember the big house, Papa, when the farmer welcomed us all into a large spacious room with beautiful polished floors. The floor was waxed like glass and I was afraid to walk on it. The mother and daughters had a table spread for all of us and for the hired men. The whole house seemed full of sunshine."

"Ja," Papa agreed, "they were good cooks and had a big dinner for us."

I remembered the winding staircase leading to spacious bedrooms. Lace curtains blew in the breeze. *This had to be what heaven was like,* I thought, *beautiful sunlit rooms!*

But after the lovely meal, we said our polite, "Takk for maten" [thanks for the food], and headed for the chicken house.

Mama flew into perpetual motion. Scrub bucket, soap, and brushes were passed around. Everyone scrubbed something. Fels Naphtha soap and Lysol did the job. Cardboard replaced broken windows, and Papa nailed down the loose floorboards. Long strips of fly paper caught the flies, and we learned to duck to avoid the sticky entanglement.

The Ford chugged along. Papa chuckled, "Mama even had me scrubbing." He, too, was remembering.

Within hours the house was clean! The large room downstairs had a polished cookstove, a table, and some chairs. The ladder to the loft revealed a large sleeping room with one bed. Mama hung a quilt-partition for privacy. Four pallets were laid on the newly scrubbed floor.

"Ja, ja, Margaret, the dinner in the big house was good. But when we had cleaned the chicken house, Mama put on the coffeepot. Now, let me tell you one thing: No one can cook like Mama—or make such good coffee."

I remembered the starched cloth on the old wooden table and the wild flowers Grace picked and put in a glass jar. We all scrubbed up outside where Mama had a basin of water. A towel hung on a nail by the door. No dirt would enter Mama's clean kitchen. With our shoes off, we gathered around the table to give thanks. We were a family. We had a home. Papa even let us dip our sugar lumps in his coffee. All was well. Papa was in his place.

Even now I could hear the sound of that first night—wind over the prairie, mice scampering about, flies buzzing on the sticky fly paper, and the lonely howl of a coyote.

"But Papa," I ventured now, "that farmer said his barn was full."

"Ja, but the wife had the key."

I had watched, bewildered, as the farmer's wife carefully counted the eggs and offered skimmed milk, a bowl of flour, and a bowl of sugar. "They had so much, Papa, and gave so little—and you and Mama have so little and give so much."

"I know, Margaret, I know. It is all such a mystery," Papa said solemnly. "The poor heard Jesus gladly, and the poor give cheerfully. But always remember, Margaret, it is the spirit of giving that God blesses—and a thankful heart, like Mama says." He took one hand from the steering wheel and rubbed his chin thoughtfully. "Somehow God always takes care of us—ja, in spite of me, Mama says. I just give everything away. That is not always wisdom, but Mama knows I can't turn from anyone in need."

"Papa, do you remember the time Mama had the toothache?" We laughed together now. But back then I had cried.

It was a hot summer day and Papa was on one of his missionary journeys to visit farmers in other towns, a journey that sometimes took several days.

Mama's face was red and swollen with pain from an infected tooth. The farmer's shiny new car, with real glass windows (not like Papa's car with the snap-on curtains), stood in the barn beside the wagons and buggy.

Timidly Mama asked the farmer if someone could drive her to town to see the dentist but he shook his head. It was harvest time and crops had to be gathered. A tooth didn't seem important. No help could be spared.

One of the hired men offered to hitch up the horse and buggy so Mama could drive to town, ten miles away. She gave instructions to care for the children. As she gathered up every penny she had to buy a bag of flour, I protested, "But, Mama, the farmer's barns are full!"

"I know," Mama answered softly, "but the heart is empty." Somehow I understood.

I watched her wrap a scarf around her swollen face and clutch her money in a handkerchief. With a snap of the reins she was off. I went back into our "chicken coop" house and played games with the children, watching uneasily as storm clouds gathered in the sky.

It was almost dark when the horse and buggy pulled into the farm yard. The hired man unhitched the horses and sadly shook his head. Mama was soaked and the wet scarf clung to her face. She was crying as she said, "The dentist was gone and I was caught in a bad storm. My precious bag of flour is soaked!" In the house she crumpled into the rocking chair while we gathered around her and pulled off her wet shoes. Silently I prayed that God would help us to get flour for bread and get Mama's tooth fixed.

Then we heard the sputtering of Papa's car. We shouted for joy! Papa was furious—not at us, for a change, but at the circumstances. "Come, Mama, I know a good dentist, a good man, and the flour we will get. Look, I have money. I didn't give it all away this time."

Mama could only nod.

"Feed the children and tell them bedtime stories, Margaret," Papa instructed as he climbed into his place behind the steering wheel. Mama was tying the dry scarf around her swollen face as they rode off in the Model-T. Papa was home. All would be well.

Papa interrupted our memories of bygone days, saying, "Ja, Mama worried more about the flour than her tooth. She could have died from the infection, but God knew I could never live without her."

Moments later Papa pulled off the main road, his excitement mounting. "Look, Margaret, there is the Thompson farm. Good people, quiet, hard-working. They have two sons, Trygvie and Seivert—fine boys."

And so it came to pass there in Canada that I stood proudly beside Papa as he stood in his place meticulously dressed in his black suit and high starched collar, his black shoes polished to a high sheen. He told the farmers who were gathered together, "Today we pitch a tent, but one day there will be a church here with its steeple rising to the sky."

I watched the big-boned Norwegian men take their hammers and drive in the tent stakes, then the large green tent was stretched over the prairie grass. Rough hands held rumpled hats while heads bowed in prayer. Papa's voice boomed confidently, "Lord, bless the world through these, your faithful children. Amen."

2

The Farm

Another day had come to a close, and the Thompson farm seemed to settle into the stillness of the night. Sounds from the chicken house blended into darkness like a gentle lullaby. The cattle and horses shifted restlessly in the barns, tired after a long day of work.

Mrs. Thompson, a quiet woman with a warm smile, patiently washed the supper dishes while I dried them and kept up a running conversation about life with Mama and the children. Mr. Thompson, still dressed in his work boots and overalls, chuckled as he stacked the wood behind the cookstove in preparation for the next day's early breakfast. Finally he stretched, caught his thumbs on his shoulder straps and peered at me over the tip of his glasses. "Margaret, Margaret, such a life in the Tweten house!"

I turned away shyly. The cows had been milked, and I had helped to wash and scald the separator. Freshly churned butter stood in a crock. Loaves of bread lined the pantry shelf. Jars of homemade strawberry jam stood in rows. Mama would be proud of me.

I filled the water bucket at the pump and hung up the dishtowels to dry. Chores were done and the evening meal was over.

The Thompson boys, Trygvie and Seivert, discussed tomorrow's work with their father. Finally Mr. Thompson pulled off his boots and said good night. Mrs. Thompson took off her starched apron and, with a weary sigh, followed her husband to the loft.

It was still early, but quiet, gentle, hard-working Trygvie stifled a yawn. Soon he, too, said good night. Papa had gone to visit a neighbor and would be home later. It never occurred to Papa to go to bed before midnight—"So many books to read," he said.

That left only Seivert and me. Seivert, the youngest, seventeen years old with merry blue eyes, seemed to be the only one with an adventurous spirit. He had big-boned, Norwegian features, yet his unruly brown hair framed a boyish face. Seivert had boundless energy and seemed to work effortlessly all day.

He lit the gas lamp on the round table and handed me a book—a paperback novel with a hero, heroine, and villain. Seivert's deep-blue eyes sparkled with mischief as he confided, "This is what I like to do when everyone goes to bed—read!" An old Victrola stood beside the table and he put on the only record he owned—"Beautiful Ohio." When the record player ran down, Seivert cranked it again and went right on reading

I had grown up under the protective banner of the parsonage and was well-versed in theology, but the novel offered me a new burst of excitement. I was totally absorbed in Mrs. Southwick's classic—and my eyes glued to the pages as the characters, particularly Jack the villain, came alive for me. Too late, a step behind us alerted us to Papa's presence. He was reading over my shoulder. He snatched the book from my hand. Papa glared at Seivert then back at me. "Margaret, God gave you a good head to read good books. This is foolishness." When he took the book I was right at the best part, where the hero rescues the heroine.

Years later I asked Papa how the story ended. Before he realized the trap I had set for him, he told me.

There were more paperback books to read that summer, but I made sure I had a "good book" handy—just in case Papa came home.

In the morning the Thompson men ate a hearty breakfast after chores were done, then headed to the fields.

Plows and horses were a familiar sight over the vast prairie, but the Thompsons owned a tractor. My eyes were always on Seivert. He was a hero to me because he drove the tractor and allowed me to ride on it. Up and down the long rows he rode, turning the soft earth. As the rich soil sprayed the air, the birds and animals scurried to the woods.

I was glad when Mrs. Thompson allowed me to take coffee and bread to the men in the field. I would sit under a tree with Seivert where we shared coffee and a piece of bread. Seivert was my first love. We talked about the big world beyond the farm, and I told him about Winnipeg, the center for immigration trains. I wanted him to see the smoke rising from the engine, hear the train wheels rattling over the rails, and watch the lonely, tired Norwegian immigrants stepping from the train into their new world. I told him the story about a missionary barrel and high-button shoes—my life's most valuable lesson.

"Missionary barrel?" he asked. "What's that?"

"A round wooden barrel full of hand-me-downs."

"Just for preachers' children to wear?"

"At least for the Tweten children," I answered defensively. "That's where I got the high-button shoes."

Seivert eyed his own work boots solemnly. "What's the difference as long as they are comfortable?"

"High-button shoes were out," I answered indignantly. "Oxfords were *in.*"

I ignored his insensitivity and told him I would be a missionary and see the world and write stories. Seivert shared his dream of a big farm of his own.

I didn't tell Seivert that I cried in my pillow when people laughed at my missionary dreams and jokingly teased that I'd probably be an actress. Papa was always shocked! He assured me that it was his place to keep foolish ideas like acting out of my head, and Mama saw to it that I read good books and practiced on the piano.

In my own heart and mind I reasoned that if I couldn't read novels, then I would write my own stories and poems, and no one would know. Besides, since I was going to be a missionary nurse and see the world, there would be much to write about.

But for now, here on the Canadian prairie, Seivert was my hero! He drove a tractor, read novels, and gave me coffee from his jug. Life was good.

3

The Tent Meetings

The tent stood silhouetted against a clouded Canadian sky. Nearby the open country wagons rumbled over rutted roads.

For days farm homes had bustled with excitement. Women baked extra bread, and treadle machines worked beyond the call of duty to sew new dresses. Houses were immaculate for overnight guests—perhaps even the preacher.

It was tent-meeting time, and all the people were one. They had shared the toil of the land, the care of the animals, the long winters, and the blizzards.

Together, the immigrants grieved over lonely graves and rejoiced over new births. For these people, life and death, agony and ecstasy were part of life like the sun and rain.

With a raw, stubborn courage the men fought for the land to yield and built homes and barns for shelter from life's storms. For the nourishment of spirit and soul, they built schools and churches. Without murmuring, they held their dreams in their hearts, while rough hands toiled long to make the dreams come true.

The Scandinavian women, with their clear blue eyes and corn-silk hair, worked beside their men, bore their children, provided food from gardens, and kept the family home a place of comfort and shelter. With quiet faith in God they nourished their families with hope. With the coming of each spring they also shared hope for a good crop, laying hens, and playful colts and calves on wobbling legs.

The long winter had passed. Spring had come just like Mama said: "When winter comes, the next thing to come is spring—then the summer. So . . . the bluebirds come, the bluebirds of promise and happiness. So it is with the winter of the soul. It, too, will pass, and the next thing to come is spring—hope springs in the heart."

The winter had passed and spring had ushered in the summer of 1928.

The children ran to do the chores so the evening meal could be served earlier than usual. Even the cows cooperated with early milking.

Now a shiny car stood beside the wagons and buggies—Papa's Model-T held a place of honor. Papa, dressed in his black suit and high starched collar, welcomed the Scandinavian settlers to the summer tent meeting.

Young and old filled the tent—sturdy Norwegian men with thick blond hair and work-worn hands, and women in their new dresses and hand-knit shawls. Children, scrubbed and starched, sat beside their parents while babies slept on quilts under old wooden benches.

Cora Salen took her place at the small pump organ. Then Papa, in his place behind the wooden pulpit, announced the opening hymn: "A Mighty Fortress Is Our God."

While the babies slept, the mothers sang of another day when all would be free from their labors.

Some hymns were sung in Norwegian, others in English—sometimes both at the same time. God understood.

The men sang "Work for the Night Is Coming" with unusual gusto, for they knew only too well the hours of toil before darkness covered their fields of grain.

Papa called on Deacon Salen to pray. Deacon Salen was an angular, raw-boned man with bushy eyebrows and a thick mustache. I didn't mind his long prayer because I sat with Seivert and the other young people in the back of the tent. Sitting with Seivert, I was glad that Cora was at the organ. The prayer went on endlessly—partly in English, mostly in Norwegian. While he prayed, we wrote notes to one another deciding who would walk with whom after "meeting." In the middle of the prayer, Deacon Salen peeked and caught us passing notes, then he thundered for God to save the young people. We bowed our heads and shuddered, expecting God to strike with lightning force.

When the deacon complained to Papa that the young people were doomed, disrespectful, and irreverent, Papa answered, "Ja, ja, Deacon Salen, but we must remember that they are here and they will remember; they are hearing the message. They will be the leaders of the community."

Cora continued to pump the organ for the meetings. Papa continued to stand in his place leading the singing. We sang, "Showers of blessing, showers of blessing we need."

One night the showers came!

Thunder and lightning joined with the enthusiastic singing of "When the roll is called up yonder, I'll be there." We sang louder and louder to the background the peals of thunder added to Cora's organ. The horses kicked and whinnied as the "showers of blessing" fell. Rain and wind blew through the tent flaps. Puddles of water formed on the sawdust trail.

Finally, Papa dismissed the meeting. Horses were unhitched from the wagons as mud and rain made the roads impassable. Some people rode horseback while others sloshed to the nearest farmhouse, their babies wrapped in blankets. The tent was collapsing.

The young people pulled off shoes and stockings and proceeded to walk home barefoot, laughing and shouting. I walked with Seivert. Papa's car stood alone by the empty wagons.

No one would forget the night of the rain. Laughter and stories about that night would fill many lonely winter nights during the months to come.

Within a few days the wind and sun dried up the roads and tent-meeting time continued. Papa blessed new babies and baptized converts while we sang, "Yes, we'll gather at the river." There were weddings to perform and funerals to hold. Up and down the country road, the faithful Model-T wound its way into farmyards, and Papa brought laughter and stories into lonely homes. He strummed his guitar and sang the old Norwegian songs. He brought hope and courage where sorrow had been, and renewed faith in God where believing had grown dim.

After several weeks it was time to think about going home. Harvest time was coming, with the golden grain waving in the sun. Farmers' wives were lining the cellars with jars of fruit, vegetables, pickles, and jam, and the barns began to fill.

The school bell would soon sound out across the fields to call children and books together. There would be a better tomorrow for them.

It was time for me to go back to school, too. The tent must come down for another year.

I sat beside Papa in the Model-T Ford, the box of clothes on my lap. Mama would be proud—Papa had had his white starched shirt for Sunday meetings. Goodbyes and a closing prayer were said. "God be with you till we meet again," echoed across the open fields.

I looked back to wave at Seivert standing beside the tractor, his curly hair caught in the breeze. "I'll miss you," he called. "Come back next year for the tent meeting."

Next year I would be thirteen. I promised to come back.

But Papa's thoughts weren't on seeing Seivert again or on my reading another novel. He was excited about returning to Saskatoon. "Ja, ja, Margaret, now it is time to go home to Mama."

I never went back to that Canadian prairie. When we came home to Mama there was a letter for Papa asking him to be the pastor of the Logan Square Norwegian Baptist Church in Chicago, Illinois.

I cried into my pillow. I knew a page was turning in my life's book. Mama dragged her feet. She didn't want to leave her yellow house in Saskatoon or her new red linoleum. Papa challenged her with God's will. Finally, Mama fought a battle to believe—and won. "Ja, trust and obey. That is the only way," she admitted.

Papa was jubilant! He was going home—home to Chicago where he had studied, home to the libraries and the throb of a big city. He was like a restless thoroughbred, anxious for the race. No one ever knew how much he had longed for the great universities, music, and stimulating conversation with other theologians. Papa was going to his place.

Mama and her children followed in obedience to God, but the winds of the prairie cried through the waving fields.

I hear the coyote cry
Across the waving grain.
My horse picked up the gait
To race against the rain.

The road was rough and wet;
Wind blew rain like tears.
My heart would never forget
The prairie's passing years.

I knew a childish love,
A friend, the prairie sound!
Wind blowing clouds above;
A country lane—hallowed ground.

Now—a dusty window pane
Washed with childish tears;
The lonely whistle of a train
Rolling past my prairie years.

—September 1928

4

Papa's Church, Chicago

July 1984

I was going back to Papa's church! My husband, Harold, eased the car out of the driveway while our two grandsons, Shawn and Eric, curled up in sleeping bags in the back of our station wagon. It was two o'clock in the morning, a quiet time to drive. But for me, it was a time to go a long way back—to the year 1928 to the train ride from Saskatoon, Saskatchewan, to Chicago, Illinois.

Along the railroad tracks friendly grown-ups smiled and children waved as the five Tweten children pressed their faces against the soot-covered windows. Papa was rejoicing. Mama was thoughtful—and afraid. She was afraid of the gangsters, the dirt, the noise—and she was sad to leave the first house of her own, her gardens, and her prized possession: the red linoleum. But she had prayed. God had spoken to her heart and she was a child of God who walked in obedience.

> Fear thou not; for I am with thee: be not dismayed; for I am thy God: I will strengthen thee; yea, I will help thee yea, I will uphold thee with the right hand of my righteousness (Isaiah 41:10).

When God spoke to Mama out of His Word, Mama believed and obeyed.

I was sad as the cold, smoky train rattled over the rails, carrying me away from the familiar to a new adventure. When the train pulled in at the Union Station in Chicago, I saw a city of a million lights. We clung to Mama in terror, for this was the city of gangsters. We didn't know what gangsters were, but the way people talked we knew they had to be bad.

The Chicago wind blew dust and debris everywhere, and the noise was deafening. Papa was like a bird out of a cage. He loved the sound of the city. "Isn't this wonderful?" he shouted above the noise and din. We agreed. No one argued with Papa.

Two deacons who met us drove shiny cars with glass windows. The Knudsons took Mama, Papa, Doris, and baby Joyce Solveig with them. The Pete Rossings took Grace, Gordon, and me. Mama whispered confidential orders to me about helping. "Be sure no one sees the children's dirty underwear from our sooty train ride," she warned. The ministry, I well understood, must never be disgraced—especially by soiled underwear. I assured Mama I would help.

The ride was terrifying. People and cars were everywhere; even young children were out at night. Didn't Chicago have a nine o'clock curfew? Where were all the people going? I had only ridden country roads with Papa in his Model-T; and this was a ride I would never forget. I held Grace and Gordon close to me.

When we arrived at the Rossing house, the fears melted in the warmth of their loving reception. I had never seen anything so beautiful. A veranda encircled the house, and the spacious rooms were elegant in beauty and order. The most marvelous thing was the gleaming white kitchen. But where was the cookstove?

Somehow, I missed the four-room yellow house with the cookstove and rocking chair. Life seemed so safe with Mama and Papa in the small house where we were all close together.

The sounds of the elevated trains and street cars came crashing in. Besides, I had to help. Like Mama always said, "Just do what you have to do." I had to take care of the children.

My thoughts were interrupted by Harold's comments about the road detours and his suggestion, "Look for a place to eat breakfast." Our grandsons, blond and blue-eyed and with Southern accents, emerged from their sleeping bags and dressed in a hurry. A Shoney's Breakfast Buffet sign blazing in the sky gave the needed motivation.

As we ate, my husband said, "I think Shawn is bottomless, Margaret. That's his third plate!" We laughed together as we relished the good coffee and beautiful buffet. Too soon it was time to hit the road.

"How long until we get to Uncle Steve's?" the boys asked.

"Not too long."

The boys read road maps and brushed up on geography as we drove to Nashville, Tennessee, where we would visit Uncle Steve and Aunt Beverly and the two young cousins, Benjamin and Paul.

The hour finally came when we were all entangled in hugs and laughter. Uncle Steve shouted, "I can't believe you guys—going to Chicago to visit your great-grandfather's church! You'll never forget this trip!"

I knew Steve was right; none of us would ever forget. Too soon we were on the road again. The hours and miles sped by until it was evening, time to find a motel. The swimming pool meant more to them than being in Chicago.

While Shawn and Eric swam, I wrote in my journal: "I am retracing my steps, going into the past—back to my father's places of service. I'm beginning in Chicago where I'll be speaking from Papa's same pulpit. Papa would like that. Next year I hope to go to Wisconsin to visit his first church, then to Canada, and finally the greatest thrill of all—Norway. That is my dream—Norway! But I wonder, how I can ever go there? Somehow, I know I will. I must go back to my roots and with going back, gain a greater understanding of my restless, impatient, independent father." I closed my journal. My thoughts went faster than my pen.

It was late when Harold and the boys fell asleep. My thoughts drifted back to another day . . .

• • •

Papa had found a second-floor flat, not too far from the Logan Square Baptist Church. We had to take our shoes off and walk quietly, so as not to disturb the tenants on the first floor. The flat had steam heat and hot water—a luxury we had never dreamed of.

I had my own clean water for the Saturday night bath, and didn't have to bathe in a round tub in the kitchen.

Mama had managed to get the treadle sewing machine on the moving van when Papa wasn't looking. She quickly put it in a corner of the flat and covered it with a fancy embroidered cloth.

Papa had insisted that electric sewing machines were used in Chicago and had promised to buy Mama one. But she knew the money would go for books, and she wouldn't see an electric machine.

"Just some things Papa doesn't understand," Mama defended as she told us to be quiet about the treadle machine. "Better to have a treadle machine, than no machine." Mama was always right.

Papa had his books and desk. He had his libraries to study in, his pulpit to preach from, a congregation who loved him—and Mama. Papa was in his place.

The lonely soon found their way to the second-floor flat. We learned to play in alleys and walk to the library to study.

Papa lived in his world. It was up to God and Mama to take care of the children in a real world.

Then we had to move! The Great Depression brought changes to everyone. Mama found a cold-water flat where we heated the house with a stove in the parlor and a garbage burner in the kitchen. The water had to be heated by gas—and that was expensive. Mama kept big kettles of water on the stoves.

Papa was oblivious to the changes. He still had his desk, his books, and his warm libraries to study in. Now we slept three in a bed. Doris slept in the middle to keep warm; Grace slept by the wall. I was the oldest, and it was up to me to keep from falling out when we turned together. The room was just large enough for the one bed and one small dresser. Grace, Doris, and I had one drawer each.

The welcome sound came each morning at five o'clock when Papa shook the stove and sang, "Standing on the Promises." Doris, Grace, and I snuggled under our homemade quilts. We had another hour to sleep while Papa got the house warm.

Finally I heard Papa call, "Come, Margaret—time to get up."

I dressed quickly. Clothes were always laid out the night before. When I went into the warm kitchen, Papa was in the rocking chair reading his Bible. I went quickly to the table where Papa had hot cocoa and six slices of oven toast ready. I ate in silence while Papa read.

With a "Takk for maten" [Thanks for the food], I buttoned up my coat.

Looking over his rimless glasses Papa said, "Velkommen" [You're welcome], and "button up your collar. It's cold." He went back to reading, and I set out on the three-mile walk to Carl Schurz High School.

My friend who walked to school with me made her own breakfast. No one was up to say, "Button up your coat—it's cold." I felt safe and loved. It was 6:45, still dark and cold outside. We walked because the street-car ride was too expensive—a whole nickel—and we carried our lunches in bags. We were happy to be friends. Life was good.

• • •

Before I knew it, Harold was rousing us so we could get on the road. "Chicago, here we come!" he announced.

The easy living of summertime at Wrightsville Beach, North Carolina, was a far cry from the sounds of Chicago with its moving masses of people, its towering skyscrapers, and the sight of Lake Michigan rolling over the rocks.

Shawn and Eric moved through museums, parks, industrial science buildings, and traffic jams with screeching cars. They rode to the top of the Sears tower, and they were fascinated by the elevated trains and the police whistles. However, the throbbing sound of the big city came back to me with memories of another day. The sound seemed the same, yet the milk wagons were gone, and I didn't hear the cries of the vendors selling rags and iron. The smell of fresh fish in the alley was missing.

While I was being interviewed by Jim Warren on "Prime Time America," my grandsons were intrigued by the sophisticated equipment in the studio. Later we toured the great Moody Bible Institute where Harold and I had attended evening classes.

I remembered the first programs from Moody's radio station WMBI—hymns and preaching. In my childhood Papa always allowed all of us to listen to the hymns and preaching, as long as we did our studies and music.

One day when Papa came home, I was doing my homework on the parlor floor. I had switched from WMBI to WLS, the country music station.

Mama and Papa were drinking coffee when Papa asked the usual questions.

"Are the children good, Mama?"

"Ja, the children are good," she said softly.

"Do they practice the piano?"

"Ja, they practice, Papa."

"Are they on the honor roll?"

"Of course!" (God help us if we didn't make it.)

"Mama, are you sure the children listen to good music?"

"Ja, Papa. We only listen to Moody."

The sounds from WLS were coming through. Papa sat up, "Mama, I tell you one thing. I think Moody is getting 'vorldly.'" I switched the dial immediately.

• • •

The past and present blended as Harold began to ease through the Chicago traffic. An unexpected hail storm blocked us on an overpass for more than an hour and turned into a great adventure for our two Carolina boys. But the warm welcome into the home of childhood friends, the "Halbom kids," made the traffic jam a faded memory. It didn't seem possible that the adorable, curly-headed girls of yesterday now had children of their own. We laughed together, and years melted like soft snow.

On Sunday morning I stood in Papa's place.

To the left was the choir loft where we used to sing "Master, the Tempest Is Raging." For a moment I could almost hear the bass voices again, singing, "The winds and the waves shall obey My will . . ." Back then I had joined Leona, Mrs. Moore, Helen, and the others in the echo, "Peace, be still!" Hagen's tenor had sounded clear as a bell and Harold Nilsen's bass never faltered. Today, many of those voices are stilled, but the song goes on.

I focused on the audience in front of me—so diverse, but all American! Black, brown, and white faces, young and old. The blond heads I knew in my youth were now white—and our grandchildren sat beside us. The bulletin board "read" Spanish, instead of Norwegian. The pastor was the Reverend Steve Hasper—not E.N. Tweten. That was another day, another time.

The red-brick church on the square stood sandwiched between other brick buildings—but it stood, clean and well preserved. The same gospel message of God's love for all the world still sounded forth from the pulpit. The string band was gone, but the place was there. Once again I heard Papa announce, "Now we will hear from the string band."

• • •

Tall Mr. Lundaman stood proudly, tuning his violin as the others came from the back of the church to take their places at the table. It never occurred to anyone to be seated before the service. This was their moment in the sun. All week many worked as housekeepers in the affluent suburbs, but tonight, the Sunday night service, was their moment of glory.

On Tuesday they would travel two hours on elevated trains, street cars, or buses to attend the string band practice. Mama played a guitar, and someone wrote the chords for her. Harold Nilsen played the mandolin, and Han Strom played the zither. There were more guitars and a flute, and Papa saw to it that I played something—a ten-stringed Harmony Tipples (like a ukulele).

We would tune up slowly. No one was in a hurry. Then, with a flourish, Mr. Lundaman would strike up the bow and the music began. "He the Pearly Gates Will Open" was the favorite. Then more songs. Tuesday night a night of music and laughter.

When it was time to go home, Papa would ride the elevated train with the girls who had come alone to ensure their safety. He was the shepherd and this was his family. It was Papa's place.

When Sunday night came and Papa announced the string band, the cares of the long week were forgotten. The string band was playing and the congregation was singing, "I will meet you in the morning, just inside the eastern gate. Then be ready, faithful pilgrim, lest with you it be too late."

• • •

As I stood behind Papa's pulpit, I found myself saying, "Somehow, I think God parted the curtains of heaven today just to let our loved ones join us as we meet together. I can hear the music of the choirs of long ago and hear the strumming of guitars. I think the string band of heaven is playing our song, 'When we all get to heaven, what a day of rejoicing that will be!'"

I smiled at "my congregation" and said, "It's a different time, a new people, varied races, but we are all in our place. Jesus Christ alone is the same, yesterday, today, and forever."

There was joy and peace in my heart that Sunday morning, for among the cloud of witnesses from the grandstand of heaven I seemed to see Papa—in his place.

5

Anna

The 1985 Writer's Conference at Gordon College in Wenham, Massachusetts, had come to a close, and I was enjoying a relaxed evening with my two eldest grandchildren, Heather and Chad. Their favorite dinner of southern fried chicken, mashed potatoes, hot biscuits, and cherry pie was ready to serve. I was stirring the milk gravy when the telephone rang.

Janice, our daughter, answered. She turned to me and said, "Mom, it's for you. It's Jud."

Dr. Judson Carlburg, Janice's husband and dean of the faculty at Gordon College, was hosting a consortium of college educators from across the country and tonight was their kick-off banquet. A prominent speaker from the West Coast had been scheduled to speak on the theme "The Integration of Faith and Social Action."

Jud's voice came over the phone, "Mom, the guest speaker missed his plane. Could you be ready in thirty minutes?"

Jan answered for me, "Of course she can be ready."

And so it came to pass that my favorite son-in-law introduced me to a bewildered audience of educators as the "Speaker of the House."

I would probably never address a more profound-looking gathering; nevertheless, I began, "Tonight you can become children again for I am just a storyteller." Pens and notebooks disappeared.

"Your theme intrigues me, and the idea of revolutionary ideas sounds exciting. I grew up with revolutionary ideas. My father was a stubborn Norwegian, and he seldom did anything the orthodox way.

"Now Mama would like the title, 'The Integration of Faith and Social Action,' only she would say it like this:

> Ja, ja, faith and vorks all go together.
> You do vot you have to do.
> It is simple—yust not easy.
> You trust and obey God,
> Love and forgive, do vot is in your hand to do.
> It is simple—it is yust not so easy.

"As for Papa, he did it his way. He probably invented brown bagging."

I saw my dignified audience relaxing. I was at ease myself. After all, it was a privilege to tell the stories of Mama and Papa—even stories of the Great Depression.

During the Great Depression some of Papa's church parishioners were patients at the Cook County Hospital in Chicago. They were terrified, not only because of their illnesses, but also to be considered charity. Depression years brought changes to these proud Norwegians.

"Oh, ja, it won't be so bad," Papa cheerfully assured them. "I come with Mama's soup."

The story was so familiar to me. He took a jar of Mama's homemade soup, wrapped it in a Turkish towel, and placed it in a brown bag. So began the daily trek of Papa's "brown bagging."

An hour's ride on two street cars brought Papa to the County Hospital. There he read God's promises from the Bible, offered prayer for health and courage, then calmly spoon-fed Mama's soup to the frightened patients. Years later these same people told how they waited for Papa's brown bag and Bible.

Integration of faith and social action? "Ja, ja," Mama would say, "Faith and vorks. It goes together."

One day during the Depression, after a hospital visit, Papa passed by the dejected wrecks of humanity huddled in the outpatient clinic. Many had been brought there by the police. Suddenly Papa heard someone call out hysterically in Norwegian.

Papa stopped at the desk, "May I help?" he asked. "I am a Norwegian minister."

"Oh, can you ever help!" the nurse said in a disgruntled tone. "We have a wild woman the police brought in and no one can understand her." She nodded toward a large, blond-haired woman in the corner. "Perhaps you can reason with her. We are getting ready to transfer her to a mental hospital."

"Let me see what I can do first."

When Papa spoke to the frightened woman in her own language, she calmed down enough to tell her story: "I went from door to door asking for work. I work," she said. "But when one resident discovered her jewels were missing, she called the police and told them, 'A crazy-looking woman came here looking for work. She has to be the thief!'"

Unable to explain in English, the frightened woman became hysterical as the police dragged her to the station for questioning. She finally became unmanageable. She was taken from the jail to the Cook County Clinic, where plans were made to transfer her to the mental hospital.

Papa listened patiently as he gathered the bits and pieces of the story. When he heard all of it, he strode over to the director of the clinic, his blue eyes blazing, "I vill tell you vun t'ing. This voman is not crazy. She is Norwegian!"

"Will you sign for her release?" the director asked.

Papa grabbed the pen. "Of course I vill sign!"

In the meantime at home, Mama had supper ready. "Margaret, look out the window and see if Papa is coming." The worry lines on her face deepened.

I looked. "He's coming, Mama, but you should see who he has with him!"

Mama shook her head. "Put another plate on the table, Grace. Papa has company."

Moments later Papa stood before us, tall and dignified in his black suit, black hat, and high, starched collar. Clinging to his arm was a large woman, her coat bulging at the seams, her slip sagging. I stared at her. High above her forehead, on top of her blond hair perched a hat with a feather sticking up, and on her bare, squatty legs, cotton stockings were rolled down around her ankles.

She clung tenaciously to Papa's arm. "This vonderful man," she exclaimed in Norwegian, "this vonderful man! They said I vas crazy but he told them I vas Norwegian. How did you ever find such a vonderful man?"

Mama hid a smile as if to say, "Oh, we'll talk about how I found that wonderful man later." (We had all thought it was the other way around.)

We stared open-mouthed at the apparition before us. With steely blue eyes, Papa glared at us, "Say hello to Anna, children!"

Quickly recovering, we all shook hands with a formal, "Velkommen, Anna."

We sat down at the table and we asked a Norwegian blessing in unison. After the meal Mama asked Papa quietly, "Well, Papa, what do we do now?"

Papa frowned, then his bushy eyebrows arched. "Anna will stay with us until I can find another way. I'll think about it tomorrow. We take one day at the time."

So Anna slept on the parlor sofa. The next day Papa took two street cars to see Mrs. Farmen, who had clothes large enough for Anna. Finding a home for Anna took longer. Finally Papa came home with the announcement that he had found a home for her.

Anna became the dishwasher in a Norwegian mission house for immigrant girls. She had her own room, and, best of all, a family. She spent her life there, productive and happy.

When Sunday mornings came, she sat in the front of the church, never taking her eyes off that "vonderful man."

The parlor sofa was empty once more, but not for long. Papa would come again and again with someone for the sofa.

• • •

My eyes swept over my audience of profound and learned educators. With my heart I saw caring people who longed to reach out to a crying world of Annas. "But we must do it God's way," I concluded.

"When our boats are loosed from our moorings in Christ Jesus, we become victims to the tide of man's philosophy. But if we follow Mama's faith, Mama's philosophy, we can say,

> Ja, ja, faith and vorks go together.
> Trust and obey God.
> Love and forgive everyone.
> Do vot you have to do.
> Do vot is in your hand—

Yust *do it!*
It is so simple—it is yust not easy.

"God bless you all."

The following day I was on my way home to North Carolina. Within a few weeks the family would gather for a happy reunion at beautiful Wrightsville Beach.

The weeks flew by and, once again that summer of 1985, we enjoyed our shrimp and cornbread, garden vegetables, and homemade ice cream. When we watched the suntanned grandchildren race down the sandy beach and jump into the sunlit waves, we were remembering our own children when they were young. It was as though we were seeing Jan, Dan, and Ralph race ahead of us to hit the beach first.

Wasn't it only yesterday?

Staring at the waters at Wrightsville Beach, past and present merged again. Somewhere on the backroads of my mind, I heard Papa's church singing: "Wonderful the matchless grace of Jesus, deeper than the mighty rolling sea . . ."

6

Woodville, 1985

The plane soared over the mountains and valleys of North Carolina. Our then thirteen-year-old grandson, Shawn, sat with his face glued to the window. The clouds rolled like sunlit cotton into the blue expanse around us.

Within a few days we would be in Papa's first church in Woodville, Wisconsin. I would be a part of the celebration of the church's 100-year anniversary.

At the moment it was enough to watch my grandson enjoy his first plane trip. Deep within me, I had a dream of taking the grandchildren, one by one, to journey with me into the past.

When we arrived in Minneapolis, we were enveloped within the love and warmth of Bill Swanson, his lovely wife Wilma, and their three children. Bill had been a part of our ministry—Harold's and mine.

Thirty-seven years ago a lonely, bewildered teenager sat in my kitchen watching me bake bread and roll out pie crusts. Bill complained that cookie dough was just as good before baking—so why wait? His loneliness was soon replaced by God's unfailing love through Jesus Christ, and Harold encouraged Bill to pursue his education. Now we were guests in his lovely home. God's big circle has room for an ever-expanding family.

Within a few days we were on the road to Woodville, Wisconsin, a quaint town of Norwegian descendants, about an hour's drive from Minneapolis. The road dipped and curved around the rolling fields of grain, past old farmhouses nestled in groves of white birch and towering blue spruce.

Mooing cows with full udders headed slowly down a country lane to the barn. Clucking chickens and playful kittens followed the farmer and his milk pail. Streaks of red and gold sent signals across the sky to announce the closing of another day.

I watched the town come into view and soon spotted the white church steeple reaching into the evening sky. Across the street stood the old parsonage framed with flower boxes—geraniums mixed with blue delphiniums and yellow marigolds. Mildred and Walter Obbink rocked contently on the squeaking porch swing.

"Ja," the elderly couple said, "this is where you were born, Margaret. Not too much changed." *Except there's a bathroom in the front hall,* I thought, *and the cookstove is gone.* In its place stood an electric stove—with a coffeepot on it. We sat down for coffee.

"So this is where Papa brought Mama, and where I was born!" I repeated, and sipped my coffee. Steam from my cup rose with my memories. I wondered what dreams Mama had at twenty-one—or were fears hidden in her heart? What dreams did Papa have when he brought his bride to this Scandinavian town?

Seventy years had passed since then. I found myself looking at the place where the stove used to stand, and I remembered how Mama burned the dress. It had been a new spring dress, not one of somber brown or black, but a soft delicate pink with lace and a wide sash. Papa saw the dress as foolishness and pride. In anger he destroyed the dress and Mama's dream. Her wounded spirit finally calmed when she learned that God's forgiveness included destroying the evidence. I could almost hear her say, "I'm burning the evidence. Love and forgive, love and forgive."

Within my heart I said, "Thank you, Mama."

At last I was able to focus on Mildred Obbink's electric stove. Mama's old wood stove faded away—but not my memories.

Within a few hours I found myself behind Papa's pulpit, looking into the faces of a packed church. Returning missionaries and ministers told of their decisions made in this church to live for God. I heard stories of young people who had gone out into a more challenging world but who remembered their foundational roots in God's love and family traditions.

Elderly people remembered me, the first baby born to the young Tweten preacher and his lovely wife. "I used to rock you," one lady said.

Another added, "Your Papa would hitch up the horse and buggy and your Mama tied you around her waist. Then they would visit between Baldwin and Woodville."

"Your Mama started the young people's work and everyone loved her readings and stories," someone else told me.

"Ja, I vas young," another one said, "but I remember you."

From Papa's pulpit I shared the stories about my parents and told about "Mama's children." The audience laughed and cried while we remembered together.

The psalmist says in Psalm 78 that the fathers should show the generations to come the praises of the Lord.

Tonight we were remembering that the God of our fathers was our God. The Rock of Ages was our Rock in the time of storm. I wanted my grandchildren to know that.

Looking into the beautiful faces before me, I told the people at Papa's church, "Papa's seven children love the same God because Papa taught that Jesus Christ is the Way, the Truth, and the Life. And because Mama took us by the hand and walked with us in paths of righteousness."

• • •

All too soon the sign "Velkommen to Woodville" faded into the distance. It was time to return home to North Carolina, where the ocean rolls across the sun-kissed shore.

The timeless ocean reminds me of the unlimited grace of God. The quaint Woodville village, with flower boxes on the parsonage, reminded me of the faithfulness of God. The open Bible on Papa's pulpit was another reminder that throughout all life's changes, God's Word is forever settled in heaven.

In my journal I wrote, "Jesus Christ—the same yesterday, and today and forever" (Hebrews 13:8). You can go home again—even back to painful memories, where God's redemptive love heals and restores the past. I did!

7

The Storm

Before Mama's homegoing on January 14, 1977, she shared the story of "The Dress" in her wonderful way. There was only love and understanding in her portrayal of Papa. She must have thought it was important for future generations, or she would have kept the story sealed within her heart.

To me, it reveals again the marvelous grace of God, the love of our heavenly Father, as well as man's frailty in life's storms.

One writer said, "We beat our boats against a current to go back." Yet I find myself choosing to flow with the current toward the future.

So, reluctantly, I turn my boat into the current to go back and take you with me to a place and time as it *might* have been. Somehow in the gathering of bits and pieces I see it as though it really happened this way.

Back to Woodville seventy years ago. Back to the year 1917 when Papa, a young preacher in his first church, raced over the country roads on his horse. He was always in a hurry to fulfill his tasks. That day, he was as restless as the wind. Cows and chickens, horses and pigs, crops and weather were the topics of each day.

He was remembering his boyhood days in Norway: cows and chickens, horses and pigs, crops and weather—the same. In Norway, after early morning chores, he had run the four miles to school, over the rocky mountain roads to the place of books and learning. Always he dreamed of a time he would have books and more books to study, and he would learn all he could.

Then that time had come! At seventeen years of age, he enrolled in the Baptist Theological Seminary affiliated with Chicago University.

Now, in Woodville, everything within him cried out for the throbbing city of Chicago. As he rode, he remembered sleeping in the furnace room and being the automatic stoker for the huge furnaces. Mrs. Anderson, the cook, had brought waffles and coffee to keep him awake.

Papa had his books, the vast resources of a great library. There were other scholars with whom to enjoy stimulating discussions and share ideas. There were museums, art galleries, parks, concerts, and people of all races with differing views.

And there was the great Moody Bible Institute with its scholarly Bible teachers, and its access to his favorite reading—Charles Spurgeon's volumes.

Papa's horse trotted along the country road in Woodville, keeping step with thoughts that went stepping into the past. He felt a twinge of regret at the memory of selling Mama's piano for books. He knew it was Mama's own upright piano, bought with her own money, before their marriage—money earned as a maid. It did not seem important that she hadn't run her fingers over the keyboard once more before he sold it. *But surely any sensible woman could see the value of books,* he argued with himself. *The piano could wait.* Then creeping into his memory was the money for the wedding picture. He used that for books, too. A picture could wait. (It would wait until their fiftieth wedding anniversary.)

The horse raced faster, and the restless rider became more frustrated. "I must have books!" he shouted to the wind. "I can't live without books! Surely there must be a way to save money—and I need a new lamp for reading late at night."

When Papa rode along the road, he stopped at farms, listened to the farmers' daily woes about crops and cows, read Scripture, prayed for the families, comforted the lonely and sick, and brought news from town to town. There was always time for a cup of coffee and for some stories to bring laughter and joy to the homes of this strong, productive community. He loved all those people and was a part of them, but that day he felt like a dry well. His usual ruddy complexion was pasty, his quick smile restrained.

He wondered if any of them really understood the time and effort he put into his sermons, the planned outlines, the research into Greek and Hebrew. Still, in church, the farmers nodded and the women and children listened politely. Then there was Mama's face in the audience. Her glowing expression never wavered, eyes brimming with pride and her hands folded in prayer. To her, each sermon was his best.

But he was dry. He needed fresh springs of water—books! That was what he needed! His restless spirit mingled with a complaining spirit. Self pity edged in with cruel cunning. Now he was angry—angry to be without a challenge, cut off from stimulating resources. And now there was a new baby on the way and that meant even less money.

Wasn't this how it was when he was a child in Norway? Sickness and death, hard work, loneliness, and fear. But he'd had his school books—his best friends. And his guitar. Even that was gone, though, given to his sister when he left Norway for America.

Papa felt empty! This wasn't how he dreamed it would be. He dreamed of greater opportunities, universities—perhaps teaching. He dreamed of challenging audiences, travel—and more books!

The horse trotted at an even pace but now Papa was angry—angry at circumstances. Angry at God.

"After all, I have given my life to serve You, God, and now I am back where I used to be—crops and cows." Sadness engulfed him. He would go home—home to Mama for a cup of coffee. Perhaps Mama had saved some money and he could get his books. That was it. Perhaps Mama would have the answer, the money. He turned his horse around, but the anger mounted within him.

At home Mama held up the dress. It was finished. One-year-old Margaret squealed with delight as Mama twirled in her billowing skirt of soft pink voile with tiny violets. The lace collar and cuffs and the wide sash made the new dress a creation of beauty.

Mama loosened her soft brown hair and danced in joyous abandonment. She had managed to save enough money for the dress material as well as a new lamp for Papa.

The long winter was over. The breeze blew softly through Mama's starched curtains. She was tired of black and brown dresses, befitting the ministry, tired of having her hair up in a bun. After all, she was only twenty-three. And it was spring.

She couldn't wait to show off for her handsome, unpredictable husband. The baby within her stirred. She sang joyously.

Before Mama realized how time had flown, she heard the galloping hoofs of Papa's horse. The door opened. Her heart leaped. Papa was home—and she twirled around in the billowing softness of voile and violets.

Suddenly, without warning, the storm broke! Blinded by fury, Papa saw only that the last hope for books was gone. "Foolishness, foolishness," he cried, "when I need books!" The rage within him exploded and the dress was left in shreds. Then he jumped on his horse and galloped away in unbridled anger.

The house of springtime became silent with only the mourning of a winter wind.

Like a wounded bird, Mama moaned in agony of soul and body. Then she gathered the tattered dress and placed the remnants safely in a chest. This she would never forget!

Moaning in pain, she put on the black dress and rolled her hair back up in a bun. When night came she put Papa's supper in the warming oven, gathered up the baby, and climbed up to the loft. With her child in her arms, she curled up on a pallet and made her plans to leave Papa—for a season. She would return to the security of her mother, Bertilda, in Brooklyn. She knew she would never leave Papa permanently but she needed time to let her wounded spirit heal.

Later that night Papa came home. For him, the storm had passed, and he couldn't understand the foolishness of Mama in the loft. At his command, Mama quietly placed the sleeping child in the crib and took her place beside Papa.

The following days she put one foot ahead of the other, doing routine tasks as a God-given blessing for survival. There were floors to scrub, clothes to wash, endless meals to cook, not only for the family, but for the visiting minister, Pastor Hanson.

Papa was jubilant! Pastor Hanson, the guest speaker for the church conference, was a welcome companion in conversation and books.

The routine order of living went on—Mama's sparkling windows covered with starched curtains, the embroidered tablecloth with dainty coffee cups, a happy child playing with a string of empty spools of thread, the smell of freshly baked bread—and Mama in a crisp apron. The message came across that all was well.

No one suspected the dark night of her soul as she waited for the moment to show Pastor Hanson the dress. Then she could go to Brooklyn! Mama would wait.

Papa, oblivious to Mama's agony, lived in his world with a new zest for life.

The right moment never came! Pastor Hanson's sermon on love and forgiveness came crashing in on Mama's soul. "Love and forgive," cried out to be heard. "Destroy the evidence," rang as a bell from the church steeple.

Across the pages of time came the living Word from the heart of God to Mama's heart. "When you stand praying, forgive."

"No, No! I can't forgive! I can't forgive!" Mama protested.

The words seemed to thunder in Mama's ears: "Forgive us our trespasses as we forgive those who trespass against us."

Louder and clearer came the words that burned into her soul: "When you stand praying, forgive."

Back into the hidden recesses of her mind came the distant memories of her mother and grandmother making difficult choices. They chose to leave the scene of heartbreak and discover a new life. Was that the choice for her also? Should she leave Papa?

"Oh, God, where do I go, except to Thee. Out of my depths I cry to Thee. Lead me in Your ways—the path of trust and obedience, the way of love and forgiveness—unconditional love and forgiveness. Only within me can God bring a new beginning. There is no place to flee—only to the Rock of Ages."

The service was concluded, and Mama moved quickly from the church to the horse and buggy, the child tied to her waist. With a snap of the reins, she sped homeward.

Placing the baby in the crib, she reached into the chest for the tattered dress. Holding it to her tear-stained face she offered the dress to God, a sacrifice of the heart. "For You, dear Lord," she whispered. She opened the lid of the stove and held the dress above the flame. "When you forgive, you destroy the evidence," sounded within her.

She heard a familiar step behind her. She turned. There stood Papa, a bewildered expression on his face. "What are you doing?" he asked.

"I am burning the evidence!" Mama dropped the tattered dress into the flame. *Mama had made a choice to forgive!*

Stunned by the sudden realization of what he had done, Papa murmured, "Forgive me, Mama."

Pastor Hanson left. No one ever knew this story until Mama told it herself before she went home to stand in the dress God made for her, His robe of righteousness.

I was the baby, Margaret Louise, and the new life within Mama became my sister, Bernice. The choice Mama made that day was the "molten moment" of her life—a covenant with God, the God of promise who never fails.

8

The Ruth Fest

"Harold, would you please help with the lighting of candles at the Christmas Eve service?" Sarah Durham asked my husband.

"Oh no, I'm sorry," he answered. "We can't break tradition. Christmas Eve at home is an old Norwegian custom." Rolling his eyes toward the heavens he smiled, "Besides what would Mama and Papa think?"

"Oh, come on, Dad, let's change it—just a little," Janice pleaded.

When our daughter looked at her father with her big brown eyes, he'd go to any length to please her. That is how we found ourselves at the Myrtle Grove Presbyterian Church on Christmas Eve, 1985. Harold was lighting the candles and Sarah Durham was smiling.

Our family sat in a row—Ralph and Chris with their children Shawn, Eric, Sarah, and Kathryn; Janice and Jud with Heather and Chad from Massachusetts. We missed Dan and Virginia, who lived in California.

We had been together for a beautiful Christmas Eve dinner in Ralph and Chris' home. After the service, we planned to return there for the opening of gifts and the traditional coffee and Jule kakke.

Christmas Day everyone would come to grandma and grandpa's house. Now we were adding the Candlelight Service to our Christmas traditions.

The church was packed, with chairs in the aisles and the balcony overflowing. The choir and orchestra filled the air with Christmas music and everyone joined in singing the traditional carols.

A message from our beloved pastor, Horace Hilton, brought the service to the lighting of the candles. One by one we held a candle and felt the hush of "O Holy Night."

The candles took me back to another day when the Christmas tree had borne lighted candles. I was remembering how Papa brought home the lonely immigrants from the railroad station to eat lute fisk and rice pudding. I could almost hear their footsteps in the snow.

As my grandchildren sang "Silent Night, Holy Night," their faces blurred and it seemed that I could hear the immigrants singing "Glade Jule—Helege Jule."

Once again I was rowing my boat of memory against the current, back to the 1930 Ruth Fest. The place was Chicago —at Papa's church in Logan Square. Could it really have been that long ago when I can still see it so clearly?

The Christmas Sunday school program, the event of the year, featured not only talent but also Scandinavian endurance. Mothers spent long nights in close communion with the Singer treadle machines, while children spent hours rehearsing "pieces."

This generation of American-born Norwegians was expected to perform before a church filled with immigrants and American friends. Mischievous boys in handmade suits called a holiday truce with the girls in their ruffles and starched petticoats and with bright hairbows bobbing on their shiny blond heads.

Against the background of scented pine, Mama gave her annual Christmas reading, "Annie and Willie's Prayer." In conclusion, each child was given the treasured bag of candy and fruit—and a heart full of memories that would linger throughout the new year.

Every family in Papa's church had a special program—even Mrs. Wiberg's Vorld Vild Girls (World Wide Girls). December began with fests and ended with the New Year's Day annual church fest. Only Christmas Eve belonged to just the family.

No church service compared with the "Root Fest" (Ruth Fest). The Norwegian "Root" girls of the "Root" Society planned all year for this, their night. Many of these single girls worked as housekeepers in the affluent suburban homes and traveled long hours on buses and elevated trains to attend Papa's church.

They banded together and bought a three-flat building in Logan Square. It was their home. The Ruth girls shared their joys and their sorrows, reached out to welcome newcomers, and entertained visiting missionaries and ministers.

No one ever told them about the plight of the single girl so they gave themselves to serve others with joyous abandonment. At Sunday school picnics it was the "Root" girls who had an extra nickel for ice cream. When they received clothing from their employers, they graciously gave it to those in need—usually Mama's children.

Their guitar music and laughter lingers in my memories of Chicago and Papa's church. Their fest was held in the auditorium of the church. The Christmas tree touched the ceiling. Boughs of pine lined the platform and window sills. The choir sang; the string band played. Hagin Lorentzen sang "The Holy City" and Leona Gjertsen sang "Have You Any Room for Jesus?" Mama gave a reading, "The Guest."

At the conclusion of the program, everyone was invited to the church basement for refreshments. (Today it is called the fellowship hall.) The basement was decorated with evergreen that had been picked from the forest preserves. In the center stood a large decorated tree. Mr. Lundaman, leader of the string band, tuned up his violin and the pianists, Eleanor, Hazel, and Harriet, took turns.

Now the march around the tree began. All year, boys had been eyeing girls in preparation for the annual march. Children of all ages paired up first. Then adults invited American guests to join the newcomers in the march around the tree. Norwegian and American carols echoed into the night as partners changed, and the marched reversed. Bowing, clapping, spinning, and turning, the church family welcomed the Christmas season in Norwegian style.

The table was prepared for the happy guests. Danish layer cakes and Swedish limpa bread invaded the Norwegian territory of Jule kakke, butter cookies, hard-boiled eggs with anchovies, and goat cheese.

The younger generation assisted the elderly, for respect was a way of life. The huge coffeepot in the kitchen held the clear amber glow of beaten eggs mixed with coffee grounds and boiled just right. Thick cream and sugar lumps waited to play their part in the celebration.

After the celebration, the "Root" girls, ages nineteen to ninety, had their moment of glory. Tall Berta Herness marched with plump, rosy-cheeked Annie Emerson. The two of them owned a delicatessen. One night, when a robber threatened them, Berta calmly called out to her "brother." The robber fled.

"But Berta, your brudder is in Norway," Annie exclaimed.

"Ja, Annie, I know, but the robber didn't know."

Tonight Berta and Annie sang the old songs in the new land. Sophie Anderson joined the march and requested her favorite song, "Jesus may come today, glad day! glad day!" Beside her marched Eliza B. Henning Hommafos, the self-appointed poet laureate of Logan Square. Eliza was fragile so she wore layers of clothes and piled her hair in soft puffs around her thin, artistic face to look healthier. She had a poem for every occasion.

Emma Kjelsted limped with her cane. Happy Synove Knudsen, slender and regal in her latest Vogue fashion, danced with the handsome male newcomers. She was too independent to say yes to any of them. Gentle Lillie Olsen joined the Halbom sisters. Marching, singing . . . they were all there—the "Root" girls with their familiar Scandinavian names.

No one enjoyed the march more than Papa. He took turns with all the ladies and sang his heart out. These were his people! The red brick walls of the church on the square were not just walls of stone. They were walls built out of love—companionship for those who were sorrowing and hope for those in despair. To the young, the walls contained the golden dreams of tomorrow and the moonlight and roses of romance.

No one walked alone! Together the young and the old dreamed the impossible dream—their heads held high. Their faith could bear the unbearable sorrow.

Papa's answer to death was Jesus' answer: "I am the resurrection, and the life: he that believeth in me, though he were dead, yet shall he live" (John 11:25). Papa believed that and shared that faith.

To those enduring the dark days of the Great Depression, Papa preached, "My God shall supply all your need according to his riches in glory by Christ Jesus" (Philippians 4:19).

To the lonely, Papa's confident voice rang out, "I will never leave thee, nor forsake thee" (Hebrews 13:5).

During difficult periods of change in a new land, Papa's answer came clear and strong from the Bible: "Jesus Christ, the same yesterday, and today, and forever" (Hebrews 13:8). "Forever, O LORD, thy word is settled in heaven" (Psalm 119:89).

The candle in my hand flickered. I returned to the present as we stood for the closing benediction at the Myrtle Grove Presbyterian Church. Quietly we streamed out to cars ready to return to the family time of Christmas Eve tradition. As we drove through the streets, we enjoyed the homes that had been beautifully decorated with lights. In the silence, I found myself remembering again that long ago "Root Fest."

The fest was over. The retreating steps of the "Root" girls could be heard in the snow as they wended their way to buses or elevated trains to return home. Papa quietly closed the door of Logan Square Church. As we walked home in the snow to our second-floor flat, Papa said, "Ja, ja, Margaret, there is nothing like the Root Fest!"

Perhaps tomorrow I'll tell the grandchildren all about it. But tonight we open our Christmas gifts.

Besides, it is time for a cup of coffee.

It was Christmas, 1985.

9

Brooklyn, 1919

It was a long time ago, yet I remember the setting well.

Standing up in a crib behind a glass partition, I watched Papa's sad face. His black coat and scarf hung on his thin frame. He clutched his black hat in his hand, his face etched with grief. I reached out to touch him. "Hold me," I whimpered. He reached impulsively for me. But the glass partition kept us apart.

It was 1919, and I remember standing alone in my long white gown, watching him wipe his eyes as he walked away.

The setting was the contagious ward in a New York City hospital where I was isolated in a glass cubicle, recovering from diphtheria.

Day after day, Papa came and stood behind the glass partition, his strong, firm hands pressed against the window in a perpetual wave. Somehow, as young as I was, I understood I shouldn't cry.

Finally, the day came when the nurse dressed me in my own clothes. Then Papa wrapped me in a blanket and took me home on the streetcar to grandmother's house. The wind was cold. My head hurt. I held my ears in pain. But I was going home!

With abandoned joy I kissed my sister Bernice. We clung to each other in a joyous reunion.

Bestemör Bertilda (Grandmother Bertilda) moved about her flat and cared for us all. Bernice and I played games, hiding in the velvet drapes that partitioned the living room from the kitchen.

Jule kakke lined the pantry shelves as Bestemör prepared Christmas. The excitement in the air was not only for Christmas, but also for the new baby who was coming.

December 23, 1919, Grace was born—our Christmas angel. I helped Bestemör with the new baby, put cups on the table for coffee, and made sure Papa had his sugar lumps.

When evening came, Bernice and I curled up together in our bed, secure in our family's love. We had Bestemör and a new baby. We had Mama and Papa. We were all together in Bestemör's Brooklyn flat.

I couldn't remember exactly how it happened, but we were in Woodville, Wisconsin, where Bernice and I were born, and then next we were on a long train ride. Then suddenly we were in Bestemör's flat in Brooklyn. If the memory were there at all, it was only a vague one—of Papa preaching and Mama burning her dress. I was too young to recognize Papa's sad, remorseful expression. Or to hear his strong, powerful voice grow hoarse. All I knew was that we were all together and Mama sang songs and told stories, and Bestemör took care of all of us. Papa didn't talk much. He slept in the daytime and went out to a watchman job at night. Mama still sang how God would take care of us.

It was many years later when I learned what had happened to Papa. It all stemmed from the burning of Mama's dress. After the tempestuous storm of anger had swept over the souls of Mama and Papa, there came a quiet peace to

Mama. "When we obey God," Mama said, "we find a rest in our souls."

For Papa, the quiet became a deep, dark chasm of guilt—and God's apparent silence. With no one to confide in, Papa rode the country roads engulfed in the dark night of the soul. He was losing his voice and the brown taste of fear brought the blackness of despair.

He had two young children to feed—Margaret (me) and Bernice—but he couldn't preach. With his voice gone, he had to leave the pulpit. He had failed!

Practical Bestemör Bertilda, who had ridden through the storms in her own life, offered the obvious solution—come home to Brooklyn.

So it came to pass that we arrived in Brooklyn. Again there was the stoic, practical advice from Bestemör, "If you can't preach, Elius Tweten, then do what you can do." That's why Papa took the job as a watchman, the guardian of a building during the long shadows of the night.

His books were set aside. His dreams were gone. Despair replaced hope. In God's apparent silence, Papa lost not only hope, but also his faith in God. Everything he had preached seemed meaningless. Each night became just one step after the other—without purpose, without meaning. Papa's Bible lay untouched on the desk.

The battle to believe was lost.

One night Mama turned the pages of her worn Bible and stopped at Job. "Lift up thy face unto God . . . Make thy prayer unto him and he shall hear thee" (Job 22:26,27), she read. "He knoweth the way that I take: when he hath tried me, I shall come forth as gold" (Job 23:10).

Turning familiar pages again, she read in Psalm 65:5-7: "My soul, wait thou only upon God; for my expectations from him—my rock . . . my salvation . . . my strength. . .my refuge is in God."

The house was still. Bestemör and the children were asleep. Papa was at work. Wrapping a robe around her, Mama fell to her knees. "Lord Jesus, You said, 'If ye abide in me, and my words abide in you, ye shall ask what ye will, and it shall be done unto you'" (John 15:7).

While the world was wrapped in darkness, Mama stayed on her knees until the beams of the morning sun dispelled the darkness and the light of God's promise broke through her despair.

She had battled against an unseen enemy who was waging a war to destroy God's servant. But Mama had a covenant with God—a covenant to walk in obedience—and God's covenant with Mama was that her household would be taught of the Lord.

She knelt beside the bed and would not give up until she heard God speak to her through His Word: "If you can believe, you'll see the glory of the Lord!" (see John 11:40). "The LORD your God which goeth before you, he shall fight for you" (Deuteronomy 1:30).

The Word of God was welling up within her soul. She had meditated on the Word night and day, and now the Word was returning to renew her faith. "When the enemy shall come in like a flood, the spirit of the LORD shall lift up a standard against him" (Isaiah 59:19).

"As for me, this is my covenant with them, saith the Lord; My spirit that is upon thee, and my words which I have put in thy mouth, shall not depart out of thy mouth, nor out of the mouth of thy seed, nor out of the mouth of thy seed's seed, saith the Lord . . . for ever!" (Isaiah 59:21).

Deep within her, Mama heard the words of Jesus when He stilled the storm on Galilee: "Peace be still!"

> Man lies before the Lord
> Like the sea beneath the wind.
> Faith hears the approaching
> Footsteps of God's salvation.

Mama arose from her knees, dressed quickly, and put on the coffeepot. The battle to believe had been fought and won!

When she turned around at the sound of footsteps she saw Papa. His face was glowing! For the first time in weeks, he stood tall and erect, head held high.

He spoke in a clear voice, "Mama, I believe in God! 'Though he slay me, yet will I trust in him' [Job 13:15]. In the night God spoke to me: 'Fear thou not; for I am with thee' [Isaiah 41:10]. Mama, all the words I have given to others came flooding back to me. I know God will guide us, and I proclaim God's Word as long as I live! My books! I must get back to my books—and my Bible, the Book of books!" He was smiling when he added, "'Forever, O LORD, thy word is settled in heaven'" [Psalm 119:89].

Papa's faith—and Papa's voice—had returned!

So that, as it was told those many years later, was why we had gone from Woodville, Wisconsin, to Bestemör's flat in Brooklyn.

Now I was remembering again those long-ago days when I came home from the contagious ward in the hospital. I was three-and-a-half years old. My head hurt and the pain in my ears increased. Bestemör rocked me when she could, but there was the new baby, Grace.

One afternoon after coffee, Bernice crawled up into Papa's lap. She dipped her sugar lump in Papa's coffee and slowly munched on a piece of Jule kakke. "Göt, göt [good,

good]," she murmured, as she laid her head against Papa's shoulder.

Terror gripped him when he felt her hot cheek against his face. Shortly he was on his way to the contagious hospital with two-year-old Bernice wrapped in a blanket.

As they left, Mama clutched baby Grace in her arms. Bestemör moved quietly about and put on the coffeepot. She, too, was feeling the fever and the choking pain in her throat, but with fierce determination, she doctored her throat with Lysol and peroxide and willed herself to live.

This was no time to die, not now. She had left her own young children in Norway many years ago when Joe was five and Elvina four. Now she had them near her. Elvina needed her. This time she would not fail. She would live! No one would know, until years later, of her battle with the dread disease. She moved through those grim days weak, sick, but with a passion to survive.

Day after day, Papa went to see Bernice behind the glass cubicle just as he had visited me. Then the day came when Papa came home from the hospital the last time—alone. Two-year-old Bernice was dead.

It was January, 1920—a cold, bitter day—when they buried my sister. Uncle Joe and Pastor Hansen went with Papa—three lonely men following a tiny casket. They walked in silence, bracing themselves against the January winds, their boots crunching across the frozen ground. One man stood on each side of Papa as the cold winds blew snow over Bernice's freshly dug grave.

The kitchen was warm when Papa came home. Bestemör had the coffeepot on and Papa's sugar lumps ready. He didn't seem to notice. His eyes went to Mama rocking quietly in the corner. Mama looked up questioningly at Papa, but her words didn't come.

"Ja, Mama," he said softly. "I put the woolen socks on Bernice—and the blanket."

She nodded, overcome, then turned to nurse baby Grace.

I sat by the window, my face pressed against the windowpane—staring up into the evening sky, yearning for my sister. At last I knew that God had just made an exchange. He took Bernice but gave us Grace.

Grief-stricken, Papa immersed himself in books. Deep within he never really forgave himself for his uncontrolled anger that might have reached Bernice, the unborn child in Mama. The golden-haired Bernice would be a constant reminder of heaven—and man's frailty, as dust, on this earth.

Mama, too, grieved alone with her face turned to the wall. Slowly, through prayer, she climbed the mountain of faith and knelt at the cross crying out, "My help comes from the Lord."

Bestemör, Mama's mother, was aquainted with a lonely, hidden sorrow of her own that was shared with no one. Always before, she had willed strength within herself to fight life's battle alone. She did so once again.

All these things I understood much later, but I, too, grieved alone. My sister, my best friend, was gone. As I sobbed in my pillow, the pain in my head increased.

Finally, a quiet peace fell over the household, the kind of peace only God can give.

Yet the pain in my ears continued, until I was once again wrapped in a blanket and on my way to the hospital. My severe ear infection resulted in a mastoid operation and many painful visits to the doctor's office.

I remember the cold rubber apron on the doctor's lap when he irrigated my infected ear with a solution.

Night after night Papa walked the floor with me, preaching and singing, until I fell asleep, until I was finally well.

It was more than a year after Bernice's death when we waved goodbye to Bestemör. We were leaving New York City and catching a train to Winnipeg, Manitoba, Canada, where Papa would preach again.

10

Minnesota, 1985

During a radio interview at Northwestern College in Minnesota, I shared stories from my first book, *First We Have Coffee*. Later, phone calls came from people who remembered Mama and Papa from the Winnipeg years. Our dear friends Bill and Wilma Swanson brought us all together around a beautifully set table for "coffee."

Again our grandson Shawn heard the stories from the past. He was especially intrigued about the story of Johnny Johnson and Bjarne Hoiland when they walked eighty miles in a sixty-below-zero Canadian winter to get to the Tweten parsonage for Christmas Eve.

Tonight Johnny's lovely daughter told about her parents and their devotion to God and family. Pastor Hansen's daughter, Esther, was also remembering with us and shared the last years and homegoing of our old friend, Pastor Otto Hansen. Later we visited Ruth Hansen in a retirement home and shared the tears and laughter of another day. She was still as beautiful as we remembered her. Mama used to say, "Ruth Hansen is a real lady!"

Mrs. Linderholm, from Winnipeg, was visiting her daughter, Sylvia, and just happened to hear the radio interview. This beautiful eighty-seven-year-old lady remembered long-ago times. Ellen Locken, as a young missionary, had been in our home and in Papa's church. Tonight she sat with her handsome husband recalling many, many years in Africa.

As the stories flowed back and forth, I heard about Papa's unfailing kindness to people in need, how he was admired for his dignity in the pulpit, and how he was loved for preaching the Word of God. He was respected for his total integrity.

I kept hearing words like, "Ja, your Papa was not easy to live with, stubborn and difficult, but your Mama always kept a happy household." Or, "We had a good time in your home. Stubborn, he was—but also stubborn for good."

"I remember when my husband was in the big woods, and I was expecting a baby," Mrs. Linderholm told me. "The walk to church was long and I dreaded the long walk home after church." Her eyes sparkled as she said, "Margaret, your Mama just said, 'Come, Mrs. Linderholm, have some good soup and bread with us and then we'll take a nap. The walk home won't seem so long.'"

I felt proud of my parents as Mrs. Linderholm continued, "So on Sundays I went to your parents' home and had Sunday dinner; then we took a nap. You and Grace cuddled up to me and baby Gordon slept in your mother's arm. We all took a nap together. Before I returned home we had a cup of coffee. The walk was easy then. Later, when my baby was born, I was too sick to eat but your Mama made custard and fed me until my strength returned."

She squeezed my hand. "During those hard days we had little money and food was scarce. Someone offered a crate of free eggs for me to sell but I had no way to get the eggs. Your Papa heard about it and rode his bicycle to get the eggs. Then he balanced the crate of eggs on the bicycle and walked another five miles to bring the eggs to me. Ja, he was stubborn!"

We laughed together and recalled how my young friend, Evelyn, called me the "wild one," when we played house and made believe as only six-year-old girls can do. Our playhouse was an old shed where I managed to organize a drama department with plenty of parts and action for everyone.

One thread ran through our memories of Papa—the cord of love and God's faithfulness. Somehow we understood the frailties of the man—the angry, stubborn man—yet we saw the goodness of God in his life as well as God's care for the Twetens in those growing-up years.

As I travel around the country, I come into contact with people who have been blessed through my parents' hospitality. The most common expression seems to be, "Your father invited us home to Mama for coffee, where we laughed at his stories and felt a warm welcome."

As I share my experiences, I urge my listeners to do what Mama and Papa did—open their homes to strangers. I tell them, "The gift of hospitality is a gift from the heart. Offer that gift to God."

After Winnipeg, there was Papa's missionary work in Saskatchewan (where I helped Papa pitch the tent), then his years in Chicago, on to his pastorate in Brooklyn, New York, and finally, at the age of eighty-three, his retirement in Florida.

The years roll into one when remembering, but during those years Mama and Papa's children were fighting their own battles to believe. Respect for Papa, the servant of God, and the office of his ministry was instilled into us at an early age. "Touch not the Lord's anointed," Mama would say. "Guard your lips when daring to criticize a Christian leader."

The Tweten children dared not disgrace the ministry, not as a matter of personal pride, but in order to avoid bringing dishonor to God. Discipline for us was a way of life.

When Papa was in his place behind the pulpit, Mama and her children sat with reverent awe. Papa was entrusted to bring forth God's Word to His people. Mama's children would show respect for the high calling in Christ Jesus. But the humanity of God's servant became the challenge for Mama's children.

After I spoke at a Christian college one day, a professor came to me with this statement, "The chapter 'Voted Out,' in *First We Have Coffee*, has meant a great deal to our students. Sometimes we have a tendency to glorify the ministry and fail to teach future leaders that being rejected can come in many forms. Even a godly man can be destroyed and not only the minister, but also the rest of the family."

I thanked the professor for his insight and for his encouragement to me to recall even painful events to the glory of God. Even in these, we are all kept by the power of God.

Looking back over the years, the "disgraceful" event of being "Voted Out" was in retrospect a result of changing social times. The Norwegian services were voted out as the people demanded an "all American" church. Some of the elderly desired the Norwegian, but the majority felt that changes were necessary. It was not the "disgrace to the ministry" that Mama's children dreaded.

Disgrace comes when leaders turn away from the truth of God's Word and preach another gospel, or become victims of the passions of immorality, or succumb to financial indiscretion. However, even in these tragic situations we desperately need men of wisdom and compassion to minister to the fallen leaders and their families—especially the children. In these tragedies, Papa believed that God's love reached into the depths as well as the heights—that we all begin again. To Papa that was what the gospel was all about!

I had learned from Papa and Mama that the letter of the law, without the spirit of love, could destroy the faith of many people. They taught me that love without truth is not enough, but truth without love can be destructive. They wanted the church, the body of believers, to view one another as part of a family who needed each other. Mama and Papa knew that truth with love could bring a healing restoration. Papa had read more than once that Samuel told Saul to "stand still that I might show thee the Word of God."

When Papa was voted out, he retreated quietly from the "seeming rejection," but he did not lose his faith! He lived in the Word of God, but he couldn't cope realistically. He was numb!

Mama, with quiet strength, went to work as a maid. Each of the Tweten children contributed small earnings. Through it all, we learned the source of our strength—God. God didn't fail yesterday, and we knew He wouldn't fail us today.

The weeks passed like the days and hours do—just one after the other. Then the day came when the Tweten family moved to Brooklyn, New York. Papa would preach again. I remained in Chicago working as a nurse.

Bestemör Bertilda was overjoyed. After all these years, her children—Uncle Joe and Mama—were both close to her, and she could watch the rest of the grandchildren grow.

Once more Papa was in his place behind the pulpit—this time, the pulpit of The First Norwegian Baptist Church of Brooklyn, New York.

11

I'm Crying, Lord

1986!

The glow of sunset casts a blend of shadows and golden light across the beautiful Lake Barkley, nestled in the hills of Kentucky. From my lodge window I look longingly at the rocky island in the center of the lake. In my mind I see a "safe place." I have just closed Gordon MacDonald's book, Restoring Your Spiritual Passion. *How easy it would be to sing "Holy, Holy, Holy, Lord God Almighty!" on that "safe" island.*

If I could row a boat to the island, then I could find that "still" place. MacDonald had said, "By laying an adequate roadbed in the inner spirit, we can prevent the hostile elements that cause fatigue."

I am fatigued.

Too soon the shadows creep over the golden shafts of light, and my island is shrouded in a blanket of night. The world around me sleeps.

Finally, I fell asleep hearing 350 women singing the Women's Retreat song—"Holy, this place is holy. Come now and feast on His Word." It had been a beautiful time of sharing with God's precious people. Now it was time for a "safe" place.

The psalmist said he didn't understand the evil around him until he went into the sanctuary, then he saw from God's perspective, in the light of eternity. I was to walk by faith, in the light of His Word.

After a night of rest I awakened to a new day and pulled back the drapes. A thick wall of morning mist covered the outside world. "But, Lord, I know the lake is there," I said. "I know the hills are there—and my island."

I sat by the window and wrote words, but my mind kept reaching for the hidden island. I wrote: *I know it is there. I saw it yesterday!* In my heart, I was saying, "Great is Thy faithfulness today, oh God—because I knew it yesterday."

Now I found myself thinking of another yesterday, when I spoke at a retreat in Palm Springs, California.

As I faced eleven-hundred black women, my white hair stood out in sharp contrast to the beautiful color around me. Their songs of praise filled the ballroom of the luxury hotel, and "Amazing Grace" took on new meaning.

Out of my heart I told about Lena, my lovely black friend, who had said, "Unclog the channels, Margaret! You can't see God for all the long hair and bare feet clogged up in the channel."

Back then my channel was clogged with unanswered questions: "Why is our son a prodigal? What did we do wrong?" The cares of this world—with long hair and bare feet—kept my channel clogged. I wanted "out of the storm"—I wanted to go home.

Eleven-hundred women listened intently as I told them about Lena and our son.

"If God had wanted you to die for that child, He would have asked you." Lena had scolded, "Who you be to tell God Almighty He didn't do enough when He sent Jesus to die for that child? Jesus came to give life—and that your joy be full.

Now I asks you, Margaret, where is your joy? Your joy is Jesus. Your peace is Jesus. Your life is Jesus—and it does not depend on answered prayer or your family being right. You must get the joy of the Lord in *your* soul, Margaret. Leave the rest to God."

I looked over that sea of shiny black faces. "Lena was right, you know. She made me realize how praise unclogs the channel and, like a detergent, cleanses the cobwebs of the mind. With the channel clear I saw a sovereign God at work, bringing the 'all things together for good!' Praise was the believing before the seeing. God promised 'If you can believe, you'll see the glory of the Lord.'"

I continued, "Our children—yours and mine—are held hostage by the enemy. We, as God's children, the church, must put on the armor of God and stand in the gap to intercede for these imprisoned children of ours. They are held hostage by America's permissive society that deifies man rather than God, and that has given the enemy free reign through drugs, alcohol, and unbridled promiscuity. God's laws have been broken and 'the wages of sin is death, but the gift of God is eternal life'" (Romans 6:23).

Now and then a dark head bobbed with understanding. Momentarily my eyes locked with the deep, dark eyes of one lone woman. *Did she have her own prodigal?* I wondered. "We don't wrestle against a drug pusher, but we wrestle against the powers of darkness." My voice was firm. "A real Satan seeks to steal, destroy, and to kill—and comes 'as a roaring lion seeking to devour' our children."

Out of my heart I told the story of our prodigal son who came back to his heavenly Father's house. The battle to believe had been fought—and won! Eleven-hundred women stood to rejoice over one sheep who had returned to the fold.

It was a high moment of faith.

The following day a message was given by another woman, a tall, dignified black woman who was known as one who interceded before the throne for the broken, wounded ones.

This woman of prayer faced the crowd with words, "When you pray, forgive." It was Lena's same theme of unclogging the channel.

With tears, the woman spoke of broken hearts and lost dreams and cried out to the sea of faces before her, "Many of you have known rejection, abuse, molestation, beatings, and rape. You have lived with guilt and deep bitterness because life was unfair."

She held us spellbound. "Many lost our innocence as very young children and saw too much sin for our young years. Many went from house to house and never knew a home. It's time to cry! Cry to the Lord! Pour it all out! Be healed by your tears and cleansed by the precious blood of Jesus."

There was a rhythmic beat to her voice. "Jesus came to set us all free—cleansed, forgiven, healed, and free. We begin again for in Christ all things become new. Cry unto the Lord! He hears the cry of the humble in heart."

Then I heard a sound I had never heard before—the sound of crying unto the Lord. "Tell it to Jesus," she continued. "Cry it out to the Lord. Forgive everyone who harmed you. Don't hold the hate—cry it out. Everyone has something to cry about. God hears your cries."

The sobs filled the ballroom of the luxurious hotel. Outside, the palms waved in the California sun while the birds sang. Inside, it was like the sound of the mourning of the ocean rolling on the beach. Wave after wave washed on the shore of memory. Above the sobbing came a lonely cry like the cry of a wounded animal. "Cry, my sister. God is listening. Forgiveness is the only way—love and forgive."

I felt my own tears washing my cheeks. "Oh Lord, I'm crying, too. I'm crying with my sisters, and I'm crying to You. I'm crying because I don't want to go back to the past. I only want to walk with You into the future, secure in Your love."

I, too, was remembering and weeping for the fallen leaders, oaks that crashed in the forest. Satan shouted, "Timber!"—and they fell. Dry rot was hidden in the heart of the oaks. Truth, not acted upon, had become dry rot.

I cried as I remembered angry Peter cutting off a man's ear in the garden. "The man refused to hear what You were saying, Jesus. But then Peter didn't hear either, that is, until the rooster crowed. Then he wept."

How many of us really hear You, Lord, I wondered, *or do we cut off the ears of those who don't listen to us?*

I was crying for leaders who, like Judas, turned away from walking with the Light of the world, only to go out into a night of darkness. How could love of money be so overpowering? And my tears were for their children who stumbled in the shadows.

I heard the speaker say, "Cry to the Lord." *And I cry, Lord, to You for the great men who sold their souls to their Bathshebas and turned to passion, forgetting the wives of their youth. Their children cry in the night.*

How are the mighty fallen so deep! I weep for those who once held high the Word of God, who walked with true wisdom, then turned aside to walk with vanity of pride in man's knowledge. Their children wander, without a sure compass for life's journey.

Oh, Lord, I don't want to remember the past because I know You have forgiven and forgotten. But I must go back and perhaps help some who can't forget. Only when I walk into the past with forgiveness can I walk into the future with understanding love.

I can hear Lena singing: "So many falling by the wayside; please help me to stand."

Tears stain this page, Lord, so take my hand and let us remember together—with love.

Out of the past I allowed myself to see my brother Gordon coming home—a twelve-year-old boy, hair disheveled, coat buttoned wrong, holding out fifty cents in his grubby hand. His eyes were shining with pride, head held high. The money represented his worth for that moment, his offering of love from the sale of newspapers. His sisters crowded around him proudly. This was Gordon's moment in the sun. Not only was he on the honor roll as a student, but he also paid for his violin lessons by cleaning the basement for his music teacher. At four in the morning he was up and out on the Chicago streets to sell newspapers.

Now he stood facing Papa with his fifty cents gleaming in his newspaper-stained hands. Without warning, the storm broke! Papa saw only the grubby hands and disheveled appearance. Papa didn't see the worth of his son. He couldn't tolerate the lack of neatness. Papa could not risk Gordon's appearance disgracing the ministry. With uncontrolled rage, Papa's hand came down and Gordon's fifty cents flew across the room.

Then the silence!

Bruised in spirit, soul, and body, our brother Gordon retreated to the only corner he knew—a cot in the dining room, with a brown box that held his earthly treasures.

The sisters clung fearfully to one another, silently screaming, "I hate you, Papa!" It was the inaudible scream of the wounded.

Papa whirled and retreated to his study. Lost in his books, his storm passed with the night.

But the storm still raged for Gordon. Beaten, bruised, but not broken, Gordon arose the next morning to the sound of horses' hoofs and the rattle of the milk wagon. Quietly he went out into the semidarkness to deliver his newspapers. Bitterness crept into his soul.

Sunday morning came and Papa was in his place, faithfully preaching the truth of a heavenly Father's love. Mama's children sat in a row—but they couldn't hear Papa's words.

Back in the ballroom in Palm Springs, the focus on Gordon blurred. *Oh, Lord, I'm crying out to You again but not just for Gordon. I weep for all the leaders' broken wives and children who have been beaten with slashing words as cruel as rods. There are tears also for the leaders, those who have toppled in the forests because of slashing wounds from family or associates.*

Words have the power of life or death. Words can make men soar to heights or can cause them to stumble, wounded, by the wayside. So many of Your children, Lord, wait for the oil and time to heal the hurting places.

I had experienced so much of the oil and wine of healing for my own hurts. Perhaps it had been easier for me, the oldest Tweten, because I became a committed Christian at six—not perfect, but committed. As I grew older, I stood up to Papa's anger, gutsy and confident—but all the while loving him. I could forgive Papa's anger because I had learned at Mama's knee to keep short accounts with God.

The lovely leader was closing the Palm Springs meeting in prayer. With my eyes shut, I thought, *I should cry for You, too, Lord. You were counting on Your servants—weren't You?*

Tonight I pray for the children who lost their faith along the road. Tonight I thank You for helping Mama's children to go back—and now we can bring the healing we received to others. We love you, Lord.

Thank You for listening. You understand. You were beaten, too. With words and with rods.

12

I'm Singing, Lord

The mist lifts slowly over Lake Barkley, bringing to my island visibility in the morning sun.

In my mind I row out to the rocky island to a make-believe hideaway. It is in the still place where I see from eternity's point of view. It is in the still place where I can hear, then my heart can sing the "song of the soul set free."

Because I sing from a heart of joy, I can return again and again to another time with deep thanksgiving in my heart. I'm going back, Lord. Clinging to your hand, I'm going back.

• • •

It was a lovely summer afternoon in 1946. I had taken our young children Jan and Dan for a walk in the park. Upon returning, I spotted a strangely familiar figure that came right out of my childhood, sitting on the porch. With a cry of joy, I recognized my old friend. "Uncle Barney," I called. Barney was a big, balding man—still a handsome romantic with bright brown eyes. In our carefully guarded Tweten home, Uncle Barney was our touch with "the world out there." Often he would wear a hat slouched to one side like a gangster and flash us an impish, wicked grin as he spun his yarns and sang his songs in his rich tenor voice.

Within moments we were all laughing and talking together. Jan and Dan were on his knee, and he was singing, "I'm coming back to you, my hullabaloo." Uncle Barney and I laughed at the memory of Mama kneading her bread faster and faster as the songs became "too vorldly."

When Mama's glasses fell down on her nose, Barney knew it was time to softly croon a Norwegian song. The tempo of kneading slowed down as the Norwegian song blended with Mama's memories of her oceanside home at Lista, Norway.

Jan and Dan clamored for more songs, just as Mama's children used to do. Uncle Barney sang, "Just Molly and me, and baby makes three; we're happy in our blue heaven."

While I prepared supper, Uncle Barney spun his make-believe stories, and the children begged for more. Harold returned from the church office and we sat around the table, once again sharing the memories of another day. Long after Jan and Dan were asleep we still recalled that other day.

"Your father was a great man, Maggie," Uncle Barney told me. "Few understood him. Perhaps I loved your Papa the most because he had the capacity to forgive the most."

A lonely sadness seemed to linger in our old friend and the lyrics from an old familiar song . . . "Someone slipped and fell. Was that you?" . . . seemed to haunt me. Uncle Barney leaned forward. "My life was a total disaster when I came to your home in Canada. Margaret, it was your father who prayed for me, and I surrendered my life to Jesus Christ. Your home became my home. I loved you Tweten children more than anything in this world."

"I know," I answered, "and at one time or another we all wanted to run away with you, especially when Papa's temper exploded." I paused. "Doris was always ready to run away."

Barney was pensive. "Perhaps I knew him better than anyone, yet there was a part of your father he never shared with anyone. He spoke very little about his childhood and always kept the deep things of his heart hidden."

"Did that explain his temper?" I asked.

"Temper?" he mused. "Maggie, I've been a wild one in my day, and I know the world, the flesh, and the devil. But I must say that I never knew a man so untouched by the evil in the world. Your father was a pure man—a godly man, and a man of great compassion."

I nodded. I knew Papa was a godly man. *But why that temper?* I wondered again.

"Your Papa never condoned sin, but he never condemned the sinner. I know, I know—you could never understand his uncontrolled temper. Neither could I." Uncle Barney looked away for a moment. "When I tried to talk to him, he changed the subject or suddenly had to go someplace. He was a restless man, Maggie. I could never understand why. He had a wonderful wife—an angel—and you children were good, obedient, and studious. None of you caused grief in the family. Oh, you were all very independent and probably could have gone in many different directions. Now, I don't understand much, but perhaps the fear of your father kept you in line until you were old enough to be wise and choose God for yourselves.

"Then again, your love for your mother kept you all close. Few families are as closely knit together as the Tweten bunch." Uncle Barney smiled at Harold and me. "You can see I love him. Your Papa saved my life, you know."

Harold and I waited quietly for Barney to go on.

"Every one of us fights a lonely battle—some a power battle or an emotional battle like your father did, and then some of us mortals have the conflict with a beautiful Delilah.

We all have our Bathshebas, one way or another. I thought I was strong, but I, too, came to the place of such guilt that I couldn't face living another day. Your father understood me."

Uncle Barney looked directly at me. "That night on the Brooklyn bridge, the blackness of despair all around me, I knew I couldn't live with my agony of soul. It was then that your father came and put his arm around me and said, 'Come, Barney, let's go home for a cup of coffee.'

"We walked off the bridge together. There was no condemnation from your Papa, only love and a new beginning." Uncle Barney wiped his eyes. "You see, I loved him. He saved my life. That is the part of him you must hold on to."

I never saw Uncle Barney again. He and his wife, Mildred, continued to minister with their special love until Barney died years later in a tragic fire.

But he helped me to remember to "hold to the good," and to leave the mystery of life's battles and question marks in God's hands.

Again, as I look longingly across Lake Barkley to my rock-enclosed island, the sun rises over the hills in triumph over the darkness. Just so, each one of Mama's children came through their own darkness to rejoice in that song of the soul set free.

When I was a young child, Mama would sit beside my bed and ask, "Margaret, is there anything you need to ask forgiveness for?"

Then we would pray together over the little sins that so "easily beset us." I learned early to keep those short accounts with God. I also learned, very early, to forgive—especially to forgive Papa in regard to the rag doll. Mama taught me a bedrock foundational truth that I have since learned to understand in even greater measure.

I recall one event when Papa's unreasonable anger was vented toward me. I was a high school student and the anger rolled up into a flame within me. For a moment, I had only one desire—to lash back in fury at Papa.

But when I saw the tears running down his cheeks, the fury in me left. Slowly, I put my arms around him and said, "Papa, I love you."

But the ability to forgive had begun long before that. As a six-year-old child I walked the aisle in the Winnipeg auditorium to stand before Dr. R.A. Torrey. "I want to give my heart to Jesus," I told him.

The reality of God's love for me never has left me!

From Oswald Chambers I read: "In external history the cross is an infinitesimal thing; from the Bible's point of view it is of more importance than all the empires of the world. We have to concentrate on the great point of spiritual energy—the cross—to keep in contact with the center where all the power lies and the energy will be let loose."

One by one, Mama's children came to the cross where the redemptive love of God through Jesus Christ became a reality. There were still unsolved mysteries, but the one thing we understood was that each one comes to the cross alone to make a personal decision to accept God's "so great salvation"—regardless of the messenger. God's plan is perfect. Somehow it comes through, even through imperfect messengers.

Each one of the Tweten children had to face the truth of God's Word and make a personal decision. At six I believed that God so loved Margaret that He gave His only begotten Son, that if Margaret believed in Him, Margaret would not perish, but Margaret would have eternal life.

Belief came to each one—for God so loved Grace, God so loved Gordon, God so loved Doris, God so loved Joyce, and God so loved Jeanelle.

That is just the beginning for all of us. After that we build ourselves up in the most holy faith. Then the battle begins!

One by one, we come to understand what Paul prayed for in Ephesians 1:17-19: "That the God of our Lord Jesus Christ, the Father of glory, may give unto you the spirit of wisdom and revelation in the knowledge of him . . . [to know] the hope of his calling . . . riches of . . . his inheritance . . . and exceeding greatness of his power. . . ."

Into each of Mama's children came a hunger and thirst for knowing God.

St. Augustine, after his conversion, saw that the Scriptures were not words to be interpreted; they were words that interpreted their reader: "There can be no holiness apart from the work of the Holy Spirit—in quickening us by grace to Christ, and in sanctifying us—for it is grace that causes us to even want to be holy."

One day we met a man who became a spiritual father to us—a gentle, white-haired man whose face shone because he walked with God—Mr. James Mason! Mr. Mason was a tall, kindly man with clear blue eyes and the wisdom of an ancient patriarch.

He wept with those who wept, he sat with those who couldn't walk, he walked with the weak. He taught us all that the power of the Holy Spirit was the redemptive work of God being manifested in the marketplace. He quoted Scriptures freely, saying, "When you stand praying, forgive."

"Keep yourselves, little children," he said over and over again. "Abide in me. Let the Word of God dwell in you richly with all wisdom and spiritual understanding." And always he would remind us, "We are in a battle, not against personalities, but against spiritual darkness and a real enemy who seeks only to destroy God's people."

Because Mama's children searched the Scriptures, they desired only to walk in obedience to God.

Grace, always composed and efficient, came through her battle with darkness into the glorious light of a soul set free. Because of her struggle, she reaches out to others to show them a better way.

Gordon grew in knowledge and the wisdom of this world—a scholar in Greek and Hebrew, successful in business, but with a cool cynicism and aloofness from Papa. Gordon's heart was still numb with hurt from his childhood. He was young when he met Christ—but he came home from the military service with spiritual indifference. When God worked a miracle in our own prodigal's life, Gordon was deeply influenced.

Then the mystery of the grace of God, the work of the Holy Spirit, exploded into reality in Gordon's life. Love and forgiveness swept its way across the years to the heart of Papa when Gordon said, "I forgive you, and I love you." That love poured out into every area of Gordon's life and reached out to bless his sisters.

A reunion with Gordon and his wife, Alice, became a praise gathering. In my mind I can still hear him singing:

The spirit of the Lord
Is now upon me
To open prison doors
And set the captive free,
To open blinded eyes
And cause the blind to see.
The spirit of the Lord
Is now on me.

Our theme song became, "Oh come let us adore Him!"

Gordon sang the song of the soul set free!

Doris, with her spirit of determination, went off to Wheaton College with one hundred dollars in her purse.

"I need work *now*, or I won't eat!" she declared.

So she cleaned the homes of the faculty.

"I need a winter coat *now*," she declared.

Doris found fifty dollars in her mailbox for the material, and while others made pajamas, Doris' home economics teacher helped her sew a winter coat.

Doris marched to her own music of dedicated determination.

Then came the day when she sang a new song—the song of the soul set free—free to love and forgive and reach out with compassion. "I can do all things through Christ" is now her theme.

Joyce Solveig, the insecure, frightened one, was sensitive to the storms around her but secure in Mama's lap. Finally, she turned to her own refuge in the time of storm—the Word of God. "Fear thou not, for I am with thee" (Isaiah 41:10).

Today her song is "Through it all, through it all, I've learned to trust in Jesus." Now she sings the song of the soul set free.

Jeanelle, the youngest, was the one closest to Papa's heart. She was the child he held on his shoulder through her nights of illness.

When the rest of us left home, Jeanelle stayed close to Mama's heart in a covenant with God. Together Mama and Jeanelle believed God for miracles. Jeanelle held Papa's hand with quiet understanding but grieved over what he could have been. Through shadows and valleys, Papa's youngest has learned a deep walk with God, and she, too, sings the song of the soul set free.

Each one of us has come through dangers, toils, snares, and tears. But we all arrived safely through God's matchless amazing grace. North, south, east, and west you can hear us singing our song—the song of the soul set free. Hallelujah, hallelujah! The song of the soul set free.

13

The Cedar Chest, 1986

At six in the morning we were at the Wilmington Airport again. This time I was heading for the snow-covered plains of Minnesota. My husband, Harold, checked the bags and waved goodbye as I boarded the jet. Harold would turn homeward to the typewriter and table full of manuscript pages. I could visualize him praying for the gift of interpretation when he viewed my hasty scrawl.

Mama had always said, "Ja, ja, you do what you have to do." For me, that was writing on yellow pads in the airports, on planes, or at a kitchen table at four in the morning! Even now a yellow pad rested on my lap as I leaned back against the cushioned seat. But I didn't write. My thoughts danced and sparkled like the shimmering waters of Lake Barkley where the rocky island lingered as a "still" place in my memory.

The plane left the warm sunshine of North Carolina for the land with 10,000 lakes, and I was reminded of my ice-skating days in Canada a long time ago when snow sprayed the air as I skimmed over the frozen river.

Before I realized it, the plane was landing in Minneapolis where our old friend Bill Swanson swept me up in a bear hug. His wife, Wilma, was waiting at home for my arrival.

She had a pot of coffee and some Jule kakke, and a desk in the corner for my writing. That "still" island comes in many forms. My "corner" looked out over snow-covered gardens.

That night Bill opened an old cedar chest. Handmade quilts and baby clothes came out. With them walked the memories of yesterday—the good and the difficult years of the past. We found ourselves harmonizing the old songs, especially, "Through it all, through it all, I've learned to trust in Jesus."

As Bill held up tiny baby shoes, we were reminded again that our children are walking through their valleys and mountains. Someday their cedar chests would be filled with memories. Our prayer was that they, too, would sing, "Through it all, through it all, we've learned to trust in Jesus."

Out came photo albums. Pictures of past generations brought to mind the words of the psalmist: "LORD, thou hast been our dwelling place in all generations" (Psalm 90:1).

One by one, each item was placed back into the chest. Bill closed the lid gently. There would be another time.

Alone in the bedroom, late into the night, I thought of life's cedar chest and the stored memories we can't part with. Then again, there are some memories we need to discard. I would be sharing some of the good memories with college students, businessmen, and churches while I was a guest in the Swanson home.

There was a time when Mama's children opened the chest of memories, then closed the lid on the "why" of yesterday and opened the door on the "how" of tomorrow.

Each one of Mama's children knew what atonement meant. Being at one with God through Jesus Christ affected every area of our lives. We had heard Papa preach and Mama pray. And we knew that when Jesus set His face to the cross

He made it possible for us to walk *into* a new day *from* the cross. It was not enough for us to give a mental assent to Papa's teachings on the death and resurrection of Jesus Christ. It was not even enough for Mama to pray. The power of the Holy Spirit made us realize the redemptive work of God in our lives; and the Holy Spirit made the life of Christ in us visible in the marketplace. This we knew. This was the anchor, the absolute in our lives, from which we did not waver.

Oswald Chambers wrote: "The Holy Spirit is deity in processing power, who applies the atonement to our experience." All Mama and Papa's children came to understand the processing power of God as we opened our chest of memories and allowed God's indwelling presence to bring renewal to our minds.

In Ephesians 1:16-23, Paul prayed that our understanding would be enlightened that we might know the working of His power wrought in Christ Jesus. What a prayer!

When Jesus was leaving His disciples, He promised never to leave them alone. The Father would send the Comforter, the Holy Spirit, who would teach them all things and bring to remembrance what had been told them (John 14:26).

Looking back, I marvel at God's processing power to bring to remembrance the things stored in life's "cedar chest."

I lift the lid slowly, cautiously, looking in my heart for a picture showing the family gathered for Thanksgiving dinner in Brooklyn Church on 57th street.

Papa was closing the door on sixty-eight years of preaching the gospel. Mama had prepared her last family Thanksgiving dinner. Together we helped with the packing in preparation for their retirement in Florida where they would be near Jeanelle, their youngest child.

All day Papa had packed his books in boxes—some to be given away, others to be sent to Florida. Mama lovingly marked her earthly treasures with her children's names.

It was late when we said, "Good night, Mama. Good night, Papa." He was still in his study, surrounded by boxes and empty shelves. When morning came, Mama's coffeepot sent the message, and the sleeping household came alive.

But Papa, his face gray with grief, was sitting in his study—where his books were back on the shelf. Gordon broke the silence. "Just leave the books, Papa, and I will send them to you when you get your study ready."

Mama urged gently, "Come, Papa, it is time for coffee."

Later Papa shuffled back to his books while Mama and her children continued packing. Papa was in his place.

I put that memory back in its place. From the "heart chest" I drew out another picture.

During one of Papa's earlier visits to our home, he sat playing the piano. His music stopped abruptly. "What's wrong, Papa?" I asked.

He shook his snow-white head. "Margaret, I just realized that I am seventy years old and I'll never play the piano any better than I play today. I always wanted to play well. And now the years have passed too fast. Too fast," he mumbled solemnly. "All my life I wanted to do everything better—to improve my English and my preaching. Ja, the time, it goes too fast."

He reached for his Bible, but he couldn't read. His eyes were filled with tears. I didn't know what to say, so I put my arms around him and pressed my cheek against his. He didn't seem to notice—he just turned to his Book.

I put the picture back in my "chest" and wondered if I could have said more—and did he notice?

Thirteen years before, when Papa returned from Norway, he had made one of his rare visits to our home. He was vibrant, as happy as a little boy coming home from camp. We sat at the table drinking coffee, and he recalled his visit to the old homeplace after forty years.

In glowing terms, Papa told about his beautiful sisters and their fine children. Knute, his older brother, a powerful, muscular man, lived alone on the Tweten farm in Bamble, Norway. Papa was proud of his family. We laughed when he told about Uncle Knute's straw bed. "Ja, Margaret, I burned Knute's straw bed and bought a real bed with a good mattress. Believe me, Knute wasn't happy about that, but I suggested to him that he should sleep in the new bed for one week."

Papa chuckled delightedly. "He never mentioned the straw bed again.

I listened to stories of bravery that came out of the nightmare of the Nazi occupation of Norway. The bunkers in the yards told the story of that tragic hour. But Knute, who lived alone in a remote area, had escaped German occupation of his home.

Papa sent frantic requests to Mama in America for coffee, linens, curtains, and even medication that was unattainable in Norway at that time. That morning as we sat at the kitchen table, I saw a practical side of Papa as he told of making repairs on the old family home and painting the house and barn. Joy and nostalgia blended as he told about getting new appliances into the old kitchen, even a radio. Knute, the recluse, got a view of the world through the eyes of his younger brother.

During his evenings in Norway, Papa sang and played his guitar and read the Bible to Knute. Uncle Knute gave Papa a black horse called Midnight. During the visit, Midnight and

Papa were inseparable. I had visions of Papa riding in the valley through snow-covered woods. He told of sleigh rides and falling into snow banks, of green pastures and spring, of birds and flowers, hills and mountains.

Every day Knute carried his lunch pail into the forest where he cut lumber for his livelihood. The two brothers, so different, were one in the old homeplace where once rang the laughter of father, mother, sisters, and brothers.

Papa sang the old songs while his older brother listened pensively about another world he would never see—America.

I had a picture in my heart of Uncle Knute sitting on the porch looking out over the fields and woods as the sun cast a glow over his world. He would never understand what a man could learn from books in a musty library, in America. Here in Bamble, a man walked tall like the towering timber of the woods. Grain from the fields and food from the gardens filled the barns. Besides that, hunting and fishing provided all a man needed. In the evening, a quiet contentment filled Knute's heart. What could a man find in books that he—Knute Tweten—didn't have? He had the majesty of mountains, waterfalls and crystal springs, animals for company, birds to sing in the early morning, and the song of doves in the evening time. Knute was content.

If there were the mystery of a woman's love in Uncle Knute's life, the secret lay buried within him. He communed only with God and His creation around him. Uncle Knute was in his place.

But Papa, the younger brother lost in his books, was also in his place.

I closed the lid softly. There would be another time to look into memory's cedar chest.

14

The Winds of March, 1973

In March of 1973, Papa's children were gathered around the fireplace singing, "Surely goodness and mercy shall follow me all the days, all the days of my life . . ."

Mama, her frail hands folded, rocked quietly and sang with us.

Across the road from Doris and David's home in North Carolina, the wind blew over a fresh, lonely grave. Near their place, a yellow house stood watch over the valley—the dream house where Mama and Papa had planned to live. Inside the study was full of Papa's books, a study he would never see.

Papa had gone home!

Mama would make that final move from Florida into the yellow house in North Carolina alone—yet, not alone, for goodness and mercy would follow her.

My heart was tender as I heard Harold's words over Papa's grave, "Lord, Thou hast been our dwelling place to all generations. Thou art God. Lord, in Elius N. Tweten—Papa to all of us—was a man in whom was no guile. A man who trusted God, stood up for Jesus and believed and defended the Bible as God's divinely inspired Word . . . 'Blessed are the pure in heart.'"

Harold concluded with Papa's familiar benediction:

> Now the God of peace, that brought again from the dead our Lord Jesus, that great shepherd of the sheep, through the blood of the everlasting covenant, make you perfect in every good work to do his will, working in you that which is well-pleasing in his sight, through Jesus Christ; to whom be glory for ever and ever. Amen (Hebrews 13:20,21).

Papa had served the God of peace for many years. Now the man who had struggled with anger as his one prevailing flaw had been made perfect. We couldn't grieve, for somehow in our imagination we saw Papa in the libraries of heaven talking with his beloved authors, Charles Haddon Spurgeon and Matthew Henry. From out of the past came the law-giver Moses, the prophet Isaiah, the poet David, philosophers, teachers, and preachers. The living Book was now alive to Papa. He left his books to meet the authors, particularly the Author and Finisher of his faith.

Papa was in his place.

One by one, Mama's children took the journey into the past with its mountains and valleys, sunshine and shadow, agony and ecstasy. Each of Mama's children came through to view the yesterdays with love and understanding instead of judgment and condemnation.

The great Communicator, the Holy Spirit, had built a bridge from the minister in the pulpit to the father who had broken communication with his family because of one tragic sin—uncontrolled anger.

The very Word that Papa preached—James 1:19—warns us all to be slow to anger. Anger and wisdom seldom live together. Somewhere along life's way I had heard that "anger is a wind which blows out the lamp of the mind." With the passing of years, Mama's children could open the chest of memories and discard the wood, hay, and stubble and remember the gold and silver of Papa's life.

We discarded the memories of how we all desired to take Mama out of the "winds of anger" and carry her to our "safe" places. Instead, we kept the covenant God had with Mama. Mama would trust and obey. God would keep her children by His power. Mama did not fail—God could not fail. We kept the gold and silver, knowing that the Lord was a strong tower; the righteous could run there and be safe.

Together we discarded the winds of anger directed at us in our youth when "Papa's reason and wisdom's lamp went out." Together we kept the gold that came on the wings of love and understanding. The great Communicator kept building bridges for us.

Over the years, Mama had listened quietly while her children opened the lid on yesterday and watched as the balm of Gilead, the matchless love of God, the comfort of the Holy Spirit, brought healing to her wounded children. She knew God could not fail.

Grace, the quiet peacemaker, had always typed Papa's sermons and helped him with his correspondence. Like David of old who soothed Saul's restless spirit, Grace played the music that was the one major area of communication between Papa and the children.

From the dark and dusty backroads of the mind, Grace discarded the stubble and remembered the gold—the trips with Papa to the great Moody Memorial Church to hear outstanding Bible teachers, the concerts in Radio City, and the visits to Calvary Baptist Church in New York. Papa was unashamedly proud of Grace's accomplishments, especially her work in Switzerland with the Billy Graham Conference. Before his death, the time did come—suddenly, like a flash of lightning—when Papa saw us as adults and expressed his delight in Mama's children. "Ja, ja, Mama, you did a good job!"

Joyce Solveig, who had cringed in fear during the winds of Papa's anger, was now remembering a childhood moment in his loving arms. It was during a seventeenth-of-May festival in Humboldt Park, Chicago. In the excitement of the Norwegian parade, Joyce wandered away into the crowd.

Over the noise of the crowd came the booming voice on the loud speaker, "Will Reverend Tweten please come to 'Lost and Found' to get his daughter?"

Joyce shuddered. Knowing how angry Papa would be was worse than being lost. She saw him stride through the crowd, pushing his way free. The anger didn't come.

Instead Joyce was swooped up in loving arms and held tenderly as he cried, "Min lilla Solveig, Min lilla Solveig" [my little Solveig].

"I remember feeling so safe and loved," Joyce whispered. "I wanted the moment to last forever."

Today, Joyce has discarded the fear of Papa and kept the gold of "safe and loved" in her memory chest.

Doris walked with Gordon through the winds of anger, gently leading him to unconditional love and forgiveness. They discarded the chaff and stubble from the storehouse of yesterday. For Gordon there was inner peace from the bitter memory of a shiny fifty-cent piece rolling across the floor. Together—as Doris and Gordon thought of Papa—they clung to the gold and silver of unconditional love and forgiveness.

Peace had come for Gordon long before Papa's death, and with tears of joy the beautiful reconciliation between father and son was fully realized through the power of the Holy Spirit. On that grand occasion, they had faced one another at the table—two stubborn, independent men—

weeping, hugging, forgiving, loving. The love of God was shed abroad in the hearts of all of Mama's children, and they chose to live in obedience to God. God would keep their children—and their children's children, from generation to generation.

Doris and I attended the James Mason prayer meeting on Tuesday nights, where we saw the miracles of God's so great salvation—and the salvation of my son, Ralph.

This godly, white-haired man, James Mason, had become the spiritual father we never knew. From him we learned that love never fails. We learned to discard the "why" of yesterday and to turn to the "how" for tomorrow. Paul and Silas hadn't cried "why," and, like them, Mr. Mason moved on to the "how"—singing praises to the God of his salvation.

One night, two years before Papa's death, Doris and I took Papa to hear Mr. Mason. Music burst forth from the piano, organ, and other instruments, blending with the voices of praise of the people in the room. These people had been set free from the bondage of the past and were singing songs that the world could not understand. It was the sweet sound of "Amazing Grace."

Papa listened. He heard the same message he had preached, yet he sensed a spirit of love and praise that was deeper than he had ever known.

Late that night, he looked at me with misty eyes. "Tell me, Margaret. Did I miss something? In all my years of preaching, did I miss something?"

He was eighty-three years old, still ramrod straight. I answered gently, "Papa, you have faithfully preached God's Word all these years according to the light you had."

"Ja, ja, Margaret, I have been faithful." He ran his hand through his snow-white hair. "That I know, but Mason has something—a love—that I have missed.

Inside, I wanted to cry out, *You did miss it, Papa! You missed the love and communication with your children. You missed walking gently with Mama.* I almost choked, thinking, *You missed the worth of your son Gordon. You missed the victory over the sin of anger.* I could have lashed out at him so easily, saying, *You never realized that the power of God in you was greater than the anger that came from the enemy. Satan wanted to destroy you, Papa. But the enemy didn't win—for you were kept by the power of God. You were kept by the same power that raised Jesus from the dead and was able to make you more than a conqueror over the winds of anger. You did miss a lot of things—but you didn't miss God's unchanging love!*

I wanted to cry it out—tell him at last—but after all these years, I couldn't say it. Papa stood before me, his white hair framing his sad, tear-filled eyes. I could only put my arms around him.

Tonight, two years later, Jeanelle remembers the out-pouring of his heart before God took Papa home.

It was as though the Holy Spirit, the great Communicator, had brought to his memory all he had missed. Then, like sunrise after a long, dark night, God let Papa hear the song of the soul set free: "Amazing grace! how sweet the sound . . ."

Once again Mama's children looked into the chest of memories and piece by piece we put the gold and silver back into the treasure chest.

With Gordon, we sang together, "Oh, come, let us adore Him . . . for Thou alone art worthy, Christ—the Lord."

Oh, so gently we closed the lid. Jesus had spoken "Peace, be still!" to the winds of anger.

15

The Blizzard

Tomorrow the plane will take me back to the sunshine of Wilmington, North Carolina. Today, in Bloomington, Minnesota, 1986, I watch the snow swirling outside, beyond the reach of my cozy corner where I write. From my window I see the blanket of snow that covers the brown grass of fall. Naked, barren tree limbs stretch toward the soft snow flurries that are already hiding their leafless branches. The world all around me is dressed in a coat of diamond-studded white ermine.

Last night I told the stories of my childhood memories of Christmas in Canada to an audience in the beautiful Blue Room of Northwestern College in St. Paul, Minnesota.

A mellow tenor led us in singing, “I'm dreaming of a white Christmas.” I'll remember that song when I get back to North Carolina. The tenor and I laughed together over the Christmas traditions of lute fisk and rice pudding. I admitted, “It is a shame for a good Norwegian like me to dislike lute fisk—but I can't stand that slippery fish!”

I took the audience back to the Canada of 1920. I told them how Papa welcomed the lonely immigrants at the train station in Winnipeg and invited them home for a Norwegian Christmas Eve—with lute fisk!

Following the festive meal, we marched around the Christmas tree singing the carols in Norwegian and English. While singing, Johnny and Bjarne stumbled into the parsonage after walking eighty miles in the freezing Canadian winter.

I told them about Papa becoming a missionary to the Scandinavian settlers in the province of Saskatchewan. They listened intently to the story of the Tweten trek from Winnipeg to Saskatoon, where we encountered an Oriental man and a small restaurant in an open field.

Papa stopped to get a cup of coffee or a five-cent bowl of soup for Mama. We children were warned that there was no money so we had to be content with homemade bread and some water.

With a smile, the Oriental man kept urging us to come into his restaurant. Papa protested, "We have no money." The smiling man insisted. He led us to a table with a white linen cloth, and then he prepared dinner for us all. My vivid memory was that of Mama being served. It was our first experience in a restaurant.

After a delicious dinner, we all shook hands and said, "Takk for matten." Papa promised to return someday to pay the man for his kindness, then we were on our way.

After we were settled in our four-room yellow house, Papa returned to repay the man for his kindness. There was no restaurant. The neighbors assured Papa there had never been an Oriental living in the vicinity. Puzzled beyond understanding, Papa went back for Mama.

"Ja, Papa, I know exactly where the place is, and I will show you," she told him. But there was only a breeze blowing gently over the empty field.

Years later, Papa told the story to Jeanelle. "No one would have believed it so we never mentioned it, but now I am convinced we saw an angel." God had sent an Oriental man with a smiling face to feed the Twetens.

Now it was Christmas in Saskatoon, where the happy festivities of Winnipeg were only memories. In the four-room house, with an outhouse at the end of a path, we faced the stark reality of another threadbare Christmas. A lonely tree with handmade decorations stood in the corner, but there were no gifts—not only no gifts, but no food, and no Papa.

Papa was on a missionary journey in the northern part of Canada. Mama deliberately set the table for Christmas.

"But, Mama, will we have Christmas?" I asked.

"Ja, we have Christmas, Margaret. God will provide. He never fails. We are warm and we have oatmeal and bread—even coffee and sugar lumps. Christmas? Of course we have Christmas." Her lovely face shone as bright as the Christmas star. "We have Jesus in our hearts. That is Christmas!"

"But Mama, we always have presents."

"We have God's gift to us. See, we have the table set for Christmas. We have the tree. We have our songs and stories—and you ask, 'Will we have Christmas?'

"We have *Christ-mas!* Come—a bath now, and then a nap. Then we dress for Christmas Eve." She jabbed at the big-bone hair pin that held her figure-eight bun in place.

"Where is Papa?" I asked.

She paused, her slender hands on her hips. "God knows where Papa is," Mama answered. Her hands fell limp against the crisp starched apron that covered her plain, dark dress. She smiled to reassure me. "A bath—come, we get the tub.

The round metal tub was for Saturday night baths when everyone got ready for Sunday. The only exception was the Christmas Eve bath—in the middle of the week.

After the scrub in the tub we were clothed in the new long underwear that Mama made for Christmas Eve. Then to bed for a nap—a ritual no one dared to break. "Sleep now!" Mama said.

We did! We dreamed of Christmas dinner, lots of people, singing, and marching around the tree. Always, there was one present each. Tonight, only oatmeal—and no presents. But Mama said we would have Christmas. God and Mama never failed.

The house was still. Mama put on the coffeepot.

Soon the house was stirring, and Mama dressed her four children for Christmas. I was proud, proud of the bright hair bow perched on my head. This was the night of nights—Christmas Eve.

Mama gathered us around her rocking chair and told the story of angels and shepherds, wise men and gifts, but the greatest part of all was the baby in the straw. We sang the songs of Christmas and I looked longingly at the lonely tree in the corner.

Suddenly the sound of stomping feet filled the winter night. Mama opened the door to a group of happy young people and their pastor, Dr. Ward. He was grinning when he said, "We heard that the Norwegian missionary had not returned from his journey, and since this is your first Christmas in Saskatoon, we thought you might enjoy a special Christmas from your Canadian friends."

With shouts of laughter, the young people placed gifts under the tree and put a prepared dinner on the prepared table. Candy, fruit, and nuts were added to the bountiful supply.

Together we sang the carols of Christmas, and once again the story was read of God's gift to man. A closing prayer followed the invitation to have Christmas dinner at the home of Dr. Ward, pastor of the Baptist church of Saskatoon. I was delighted! We always had the lonely people to our house and now we were invited out as "company."

Their retreating steps echoed in the snow. Mama's face was shining. Her faith had been rewarded. *She had known we would have Christmas!*

We rushed into action—the butter, salt, and pepper, water in the glasses, roast chicken, even cranberry sauce there was no end to delicacies—cookies, fruit cake. But best of all, no lute fisk!

Then we heard another sound of crunching footsteps in the snow—just outside the door. The door burst open and there stood Papa! His place was already set at the table. "Faith and works go together," Mama said.

Papa rubbed his cold hands to warm them. "I was lost in a blizzard—but now I am home—safe and warm," he said.

The joy of Christmas filled the house with laughter and songs. Faith filled my heart. Late into the night we listened to Papa's story of how he was lost in a blizzard.

His eyes sparkled. "The snow swirled around me in blinding fury while the wind beat against me. I was all alone, lost in a world of white. I stood still—then I cried to the Lord. 'God, I am lost, but You aren't lost. You know where I am. Please guide me to a safe place.'"

With awe in his voice, Papa told how a warm presence drew close and he followed the warmth to a cabin nearly covered by snow. There he stayed and helped the pioneer family shovel a path to the barn. He helped milk the cow, gather eggs, and cut wood for the stove. The family and Papa cared for each other until the storm passed.

• • •

I paused for a moment as I looked over my audience—handsome businessmen and their beautifully dressed wives.

The room glowed with candlelight, the people sipped cranberry punch. Then I continued. "During the winter storms in Colorado when my husband, Harold, was a boy, his mother warned, 'Don't cut across the open fields but follow the fence along the road to school.'

"Harold and the other children trudged to school through the high snow drifts, staying close to the fence all the way. No one dared to blaze a short cut through the open fields." I leaned forward, closer to my audience. "We face many blizzards in life—broken relationships, broken dreams, losses, and tragedy. Life's blizzards come, and we feel trapped by the storms swirling around us."

The smartly dressed businessman directly in front of me twirled his glass of cranberry punch. I watched him as I said, "My father cried out to God, 'I'm lost.'"

The man looked up and nodded. My gaze swept across the room to other faces. "Jesus speaks to us across the storms of life and warns, 'Don't take a short cut across the fields of man's philosophy. Stay close to the fence—the marker—the way.' For remember, Jesus said, 'I am the way!'"

I paused, looking at the flickering candles on the tables. There was a warm glow in my heart when I told them, "Out of the past I seem to hear Papa say, 'I was lost, but God brought me home . . . not only home to Mama and the children on Christmas Eve but also home to God.

16

Songs in the Night

It was 1975 when Mama and her daughters stood beside the second grave on the hill. The wind cried in the valley as another sound echoed from the courts of heaven—the sound of a soul set free. Our brother, Gordon, had been cut down in the prime of his life by an aneurysm. The reunion between father and son was now complete. Through our heartache and tears, we joined in singing, "Amazing grace! how sweet the sound . . ."

Like Papa, Gordon had a restless nature, an unquenchable thirst for knowledge and a bent toward independence. He was an intellectual man—a man who could be both cynical and compassionate, stubborn and gentle. He was a good friend, a hard worker, a man given to laughter, and a man consumed with goals. Gordon had an unending love for books and music, New York City, and his wife and children. He was also Mama's "boy" and a brother adored by his sisters. But for years a distance existed between Papa and Gordon—father and son. Finally the seeds of faith that had been planted in Gordon in childhood—and had always been part of him—burst forth in his adulthood. He became a spiritual giant—a man who experienced and extended unconditional love and forgiveness. Gordon became what he had always been deep inside—a man with a warm, responsive heart.

If God had given us the choice, we would have said, "It's too soon, Lord. He's too young." But deep within we knew that Gordon was free—at home with his Savior and walking the courts of heaven with Papa. We could not ask for more.

Gordon Lund Tweten
The sound of taps across the hill,
A silent pause,
And the world is still.
A swaying branch of scented pine,
Gentle breezes
Over the hills of time.
Light fills the glory of the dawn,
Eternal Home!
Glorious sunrise—earth's shadows gone!
Worship and praise around the throne,
Hallelujahs ring,
Worthy, worthy, worthy is my King.

"The blanket of snow covers the bleakness of winter," Mama had always said, "but when winter comes, the next thing to come is spring." Just so, the blanket of God's love covers the bleakness of sad memories. Mama had only a year-and-a-half—just one springtime left—after Gordon's homegoing.

On January 16, 1977, at two o'clock in the afternoon—with a blanket of snow outside covering the bleakness of winter—we gathered to say goodbye to Mama. The quiet memorial service defied the blizzard raging on the other side of the church walls. "Let not your heart be troubled" once again sounded across the pages of time.

A settled faith lingered in the hearts of the five sisters, Mama's daughters. We followed her gray casket into the icy wind—so reminiscent of the Canadian winters.

We buried Mama beside Papa and Gordon. The two older graves were covered with snow. Bundled in coats and scarves, we braced ourselves against the wind and huddled together around Mama's open grave.

Across the road Mama's yellow house stood empty and silent, the coffeepot cold.

Slowly we walked to Doris and David's big house where logs blazed with warmth, and the coffee was hot. An amber glow of love engulfed us. We knew that Mama was safe in the house of the Lord forever. The restless stream, Papa, and the flowing river, Mama, were eternally united by God's amazing grace.

Papa, Mama, and Gordon—all in their place.

The winter of the soul will pass. The next thing to come is spring for "some golden daybreak, Jesus will come!" Then we shall see Him face to face.

Dear Lord,

"Please take our reservation.
Mark down the time and place
Where we may walk together
And talk face to face.
We know there will be many
Singing of Your grace,
But—take our reservation.
Mark down our time and place."

—Margaret, Grace, Doris,
Joyce Solveig, Jeanelle

17

Papa's Bible

I am home again where the sun shines on the pampas grass and the ocean rolls over the sandy shore. The Minnesota snow is a fading memory. But the love and warmth of friends stay gently on my mind.

This morning my "still" place is the kitchen with my books and yellow legal pages strewn over the table. It is early and the world is asleep, but my coffeepot is awake.

In my hands I hold two books. One is my father's Norwegian Bible, the other, his Norwegian songbook, *Evangelisten.* The note in the Bible says:

> Dear Margaret,
>
> This is for you, in loving memory of your father.
>
> Love, Mother, 1973.

Turning the yellow pages of the songbook, I read the words of the familiar lullaby that I used with our children. Now I sing the same song to my grandchildren:

> "Sangen om Jesus
> Syng den igjen, igjen."
> [Songs about Jesus, sing them again and again.]

Sermon notes are tucked between the pages of the Bible and songbook. Some are written in Norwegian, others in English. My childhood language returns with the help of a Norwegian dictionary as I look at one of Papa's sermons on the "Grace of God and Reasons to Believe." The sermon closes with Romans 11:33: "O the depth of the riches both of the wisdom and knowledge of God! How unsearchable are his judgments, and his ways past finding out!"

I reach for the books on my shelf—Papa's worn *Treasury of David.* (It has taken me four years to get to Spurgeon's fourth volume.) The marked pages in Spurgeon's read, "The Bible should be our Mentor, Monitor, our Memento Mori, our Remembrance and the keeper of our conscience."

My sister Joyce Solveig has a favorite picture of Papa, with his snow-white head bent over the open Bible. My mental picture is one of Papa meticulously dressed in his striped trousers, swallow tail coat and high, starched collar. (Mama alone ironed Papa's starched shirt for Sundays.)

When Papa stood behind the pulpit and opened his Bible, it was with a sense of awe that Mama and her children knew that Papa was in his place. To Papa, the pulpit was the sacred place from which mortal man proclaimed, "Thus saith the Lord."

It is through this memory that Mama's children are able to leave the quicksand of human speculation as to the why of Papa's winds of anger. From this we are able to move to the higher ground of God's divine love and matchless grace.

To all of us who have been wounded by winds of anger, in whatever form the storms come, there is only one place of surety—the cross. "The cross," according to Oswald Chambers, "is the point where God and sinful man merge with a crash, and the way to life is opened—but the crash is on the heart of God." Only at the cross can we realize how much we have been forgiven; then we can cry out, "I forgive as I have been forgiven."

In Harry Dent's book *Cover Up* he deals with the Watergate in all of us, the desire to cover up. For me, it would have been easy to cover the winds of anger, but in my travels I have heard the cries of many who have been wounded by life's storms. The storms of anger can damage all of us, but the stagnant pool of *unforgiveness* will *destroy us.*

Only when we are uncovered to the grace of God can we be covered by the love of God. There is no firmer ground than forgiveness.

All through the pages of Papa's sermons I read the message of God's grace and mercy—and "God is faithful." Today I finally see Papa as a man hungry for God, the way God must have seen him. Yesterday, I saw only the storm in the man.

Through the ages God's perfect plan has been carried out through imperfect people. Looking through the notes, I smiled at Papa's three-point sermons. One caught my attention:

> *A Formula for Duty Living:*
>
> 1. Prayer—Motivating force.
> 2. Pluck—Impelling force.
> 3. Perspiration—Accomplishing force.

I think back, remembering the day when Papa took me to Paul Rader's tabernacle in Chicago to hear Gypsy Smith. "Listen to Gypsy Smith's words, Margaret," Papa told me. "He paints pictures with words like an artist paints with oil. Every time I hear Gypsy Smith he makes the gospel fresh and new. Margaret, we must never lose the wonder of the cross."

I read from the marked Spurgeon volume: "It is not enough to read the Bible. Meditation assists the memory to lock up the jewels of divine truth in her treasury. It has the digesting power to turn special truth into nourishment. It helps to renew the heart to grow upward and increase in power to know the things freely given of God."

Again I am reminded that we must act upon truth, or it becomes dry rot within us.

While I was sorting through Papa's papers, the phone rang. It was Monroe Holvick, an old friend of the family. After their fifty-one years of a happy marriage, his wife Leona had died at the age of ninety-two. Monroe was remembering their years as rural American Sunday school missionaries.

"I was led to the Lord in your father's church," Monroe choked, "and your father baptized me and married Leona and me."

Moments later he said, "Leona and I read *First We Have Coffee* three times and we laughed and cried together, remembering many happy hours in your home."

"Monroe, tell me, what do you remember the most about my father? I'm writing a sequel to *First We Have Coffee,* a book called *Papa's Place.*

"Oh, how wonderful! Your father? The Bible, Margaret. He was a man with the Book. How he loved the Word of God!"

"Did you remember his explosive temper?"

A quiet pause followed, then gently Monroe answered, "I loved him too much to remember that part. I only remember how much your Papa loved God and people in need. Every time he preached, we went home with something to remember."

Kindly he added, "Even Moses had a temper, Margaret."

When our conversation ended, I realized again how much love covers and I prayed, "Lord, help me to see others through eyes of love, rather than judgment."

I reach into Papa's sermon notes again and see this:

Amazing Love:

1. Nature.
2. Object.
3. Gift.
4. Blessing.
5. Terms laid down by God.

How Papa loved oratory! He practiced for hours to improve his English. His notes to himself read:

1. Don't argue—persuade.
2. Move toward a decision.
3. Have a key sentence.
4. Phrase with care—phrase simply.

The more I read, the more I realize what a great teacher he would have been. From my perspective now, I can visualize him in a classroom fulfilling his lifelong dream—teaching all that was stored up inside of him.

In one of his wistful moods, I recall how Papa told me that he had a secret dream to go to a great university and get his doctorate in theology. But someone had suggested that he was needed to minister to the Scandinavian people. The dream was buried.

Was he thinking of that dream as he prepared for his ordination? He had written: "Man comes to a sense of his own greatness only after he has humbled himself in the dust before the majesty of God. God does not want man to obey out of fear and cringe before Him. He wants man to stand up, a new creation in Christ, and God can speak to him. Man must stand erect, girt and ready to obey. There is no room for pride, since we are not our own. All power is given."

Perfection was important to Papa. I recall how angry he became when we didn't enunciate words properly. "Speak up! Stand up straight! Look people in the eye when you shake hands!" he told us. Now I can smile, but it wasn't humorous at the time.

"Go polish your shoes! Brush your hair! Don't disgrace the ministry!" It was always "the ministry."

I continue reading from Papa's notes: "People can only be induced willingly to do what they want to do. A good speaker clears the mind of the audience from previous thoughts; then the hearer can be introduced to your message."

When I turn the page, I read:

1. How do you go on when no one is listening?
2. Why am I sent to work where circumstances are adverse?
3. Am I merely a man exposed to conflict, pain, and failure?

Papa answered his own questions, saying, "The answer is that life is a campaign, not a holiday. We go on because a prophet is sent by God with a message. It is in the battle where we prove our mettle."

At this point I stop to ask myself the questions, *Do I really listen? Do I wait to hear from God before I speak? Do I hear what people really say, or do I hear words?* And then I pray, "Spirit of the living God, fall fresh on me."

In the morning stillness I turn to Psalm 18, where David remembers the blessings of the Lord. Spurgeon suggests that, like David of old, we should publish abroad the story of the covenant of the cross, the Father's election, the Son's redemption, and the Spirit's regeneration. Write a memorial of

God's mercies he says, not only for our comfort, but for our children and grandchildren. Then our children will also rejoice in the Lord. In the margin I wrote: "Take heart, Margaret, and write (May 1982)."

Somehow it seems that I am discovering Papa's depth, touching his soul as I read his sermon notes.

Sins of Civilization:

1. Spiritual ingratitude.
2. Moral corruption.
3. Spiritual pride.
4. Ecclesiastical complacency.

Beside the four points, he had written: "There can be no religion where human rights are not recognized. The day of Jehovah is a day of searching—judgement. We could change human lives by persuading them to believe that by the grace of God their lives could be changed."

Over and over Papa wrote his sermon points, asked heart-searching questions and writing down his answers.

Knowledge of God Gained From:

1. Notice.
2. Scripture.
3. Observation.
4. Experience.

"Son of man," Papa wrote, "stand upon your feet! *Why?* 1. God asks you to. 2. You are a man—erect. 3. God wants to speak to you. 4. So—listen. 5. Look. 6. Go. 7. Prove yourself a man."

Great expository preachers inspired Papa, men like G. Campbell Morgan. According to *A School of Christ* by Nathan Wood, Morgan's weekly convocation lectures at Gordon College, Wenham, Massachusetts, in 1920–1931 are remembered as some of his greatest work. Morgan left a lasting impression on eight generations of Gordon students. He brought an example of expository preaching with vivid phrasing, logic, and diction and a voice ranging from confidential whispers to deep, organlike tones.

Dr. Harry A. Ironside, another man Papa admired, completed the exposition of the entire Bible during his seventeen years as pastor of the great Moody Memorial Church in Chicago.

Perhaps because Papa never reached his own theological goals, he wanted us to hear great preaching from outstanding men of God like Dr. R.A. Torrey, Dr. Harry A. Ironside, Dr. Will Houghton, and Dr. V. Raymond Edmman. Papa greatly admired Dr. Scarborough and Dr. R.G. Lee from the South and Dr. William Ward Ayer, the pastor of New York City's Calvary Baptist Church.

When the young men came on the scene, Papa rejoiced to see the great evangelistic emphasis by Dr. Torrey Johnson, founder of Youth for Christ; Dr. Robert Cook, president of King's College; and Billy Graham.

During Billy Graham's first New York Crusade, Papa was deeply moved. Later he told me, "I found myself weeping as I watched humanity coming like mountain streams from the balcony and moving toward the river of life. Margaret, I'll never forget what I saw—with my own eyes. The simple message of the gospel is still the power of God to change lives."

As I read Papa's notes, I see his struggles and convictions. "When the hearer in the pew hears from the pulpit 'Thus saith the Lord,' he has a choice to make. Either the hearer chooses to obey or he chooses to disobey."

Again he wrote: "Obedience to truth is the simple way. Most of us know what to do, but would rather spend hours discussing the *why* of the situation, rather than obey God's *how* to move to higher spiritual ground. So simple—just not easy."

Mama's quiet walk of obedience brought a steadying factor into a household's encounter with "storms." God had His own way of weaving a tapestry of "all things" for good.

When I recall bits and pieces of conversations with Papa, I can now sense his frustration at being ahead of his time. He was hemmed into one sphere of service when his outlook was ecumenical. He longed for the fellowship of all believers in Christ, longed to escape being bound by diverse doctrinal barriers.

Today I see the crumbling of the divisive wall, and I rejoice in the fellowship of "oneness in Christ Jesus."

How Papa would rejoice to see me tell the old story of Jesus and His love to a Catholic audience, and then share the same message in a Baptist church.

In a formal setting of robes and candles, I tell the simplicity of "God so loved the world," and we kneel together. In the informal setting of drums and guitars, we also praise the Lord together.

Someone once came to me and said, "You are doing all the things that were in your father's heart to do." (Thank You, Lord!)

Then there was the night when seven thousand people at the Booksellers Convention gathered in Kennedy Center to praise God. When we stood together, representing all denominations, and sang the Hallelujah Chorus, I thought the heavens would open. (Didn't I hear Papa shouting all over God's heaven?)

I close Papa's Bible and put his journal notes and songbook away. I have just had a fresh glimpse of Papa—a glimpse of his own searching heart—a glimpse that poured a fresh healing balm on my own memories. I sense his frustrations, his insatiable quest for books, his unfinished theological dreams and goals.

I had seen Papa stretching tiptoe toward his God, and I had seen him silently weeping, struggling with his winds of anger. A proud man. A godly man.

From his journals, I knew him with a new intensity. How much Papa had loved God and Mama and his children. Again I realized that Papa had bypassed his own childhood. He was a boy grown up too soon—a young man thrust into responsibility before his time. Papa had suffered great losses as a child—his siblings, his parents. At seventeen, he had struck out alone for America.

In Mama and in his God, Papa had found strength and sure-footing. In his books and in his preaching he had found acceptance. One thing I knew as I closed his journals—something I had always known—Papa loved his children. Perhaps he left the rearing of the children to Mama in order to keep a safe distance, to veil his fear of losing us as he had lost his siblings and my younger sister, Bernice. From his children he had sought perfection, demanded it. But from his journals I knew that Papa, too, had sought to be God's perfect man.

Somehow it seems that Papa must be looking over my shoulder, saying, "Ja, ja, Margaret, so you are reading my notes!" I can almost hear him chuckle. "Ja, now maybe you will listen."

Then again I can almost see him with a tear in his eye. "Someday, Margaret, we'll talk it over. It is good to write the joy and sorrow of life. But above all else, write about God's grace and mercy."

18

The Road Home

On October 2, 1986, at seven in the evening, my husband, my daughter, and I settled back in our seats, fastened our seat belts, and prepared for take-off from the Boston airport: final destination—Papa's homeplace.

We were on our way! But the first stop would be Frankfurt, Germany, to attend the International Book Fair.

It was like a dream. Janice, Harold, and I were drinking coffee on the Lufthansa Airline, while efficient flight attendants passed out delicious German pastries. Now there was time to relax and laugh at our mad scramble to get ready. Delayed passports, the air flight from North Carolina, and too much baggage all were a part of our departure.

Janice, our expert travel agent, had made all the arrangements—planes, trains, and hotels. I settled back for a long nap.

As dawn came up over the ocean, we landed in the German airport of Frankfurt. A babble of strange voices and sounds surrounded us. It was then I knew how Papa felt when he landed at Ellis Island when he was only seventeen.

In the crowd we spotted Linda and John Crone from Here's Life Publishers. They were waiting with flowers and a camera. John's camera flashed, catching our look of bewilderment on film—then, snapping our joy of recognition.

With people and baggage crammed into the car, John wended his way through traffic to a quaint village. The guest house looked like a picture postcard. Lace curtains and window boxes with flowers looked out over a courtyard of gardens.

The cheerful rooms, and their feather beds, offered a welcome rest after the all-night flight.

The International Book Fair consisted of seven vast buildings of beautiful marble, glass, and tile. Publishers from around the world displayed their latest publications in decorated booths. We were only one of the two hundred thousand visitors passing through the buildings that day.

Buildings with books! How Papa would have enjoyed the Book Fair. The religious publishers had their booths in a separate building. It was in this building that Here's Life Publishers had their display. As we passed the various booths, we heard a number of different languages but the message was always the same.

The Germans hosted a beautiful banquet for the evangelical publishers. As director of Women's Ministry in Grace Chapel, Lexington, Massachusetts, Janice believed that women's vision of the world could be enlarged through the exchange of ideas from worldwide publishers.

At the close of the Sunday morning worship service, we stood to offer the Lord's prayer—each one in his own language.

Reluctantly, we said goodbye to Linda and John and the beautiful city of Frankfurt, and we boarded a train for the twelve-hour ride to Copenhagen, Denmark.

When we arrived and were settled in the hotel, we contacted Harold's family and took a cab to the home of Bodil

Krogh, his gracious eighty-four-year-old cousin. Her white hair framed a delicate face with laughing blue eyes—a perfect reminder of Harold's beautiful mother.

Bodil opened an album that held a record of her American family. Later, at her only son's home, we sat at a table set with exquisite Copenhagen china, along with flowers and candles. Small American and Danish flags decorated each place setting. We joined hands and Harold prayed God's blessing on his Danish family. We left with tears of joy, knowing that we would meet again.

Before boarding the train for Stockholm, Sweden, our next stop en route to Papa's place, we arranged a tour of the beautiful city of Copenhagen that included seeing the Little Mermaid, the changing of the guard at the palace, a walk down the famous "walking street," where shoppers walk "bumper to bumper," and the renowned Copenhagen Circus.

In Sweden, we spent the night at the Royal Viking with its crystal staircase. High tea at four o'clock included magnificent music by a lovely young harpist and tea with delicacies served by Swedish girls who spoke fluent English.

We were walking in a new world. Even the European breakfast was a delight with its boiled eggs, rolls, dark bread, and platters artistically arranged with assorted cheeses, ham, and fish, served with strong coffee and rich cream.

The European trains, the hotels, the restaurants, shopping, civic events, the Stockholm symphony—we walked to them all, crowding them all in.

Finally with growing anticipation, we boarded the train for Oslo, Norway, where Bjorne and Rut Langmo met us and opened their lovely home to us. We went everywhere together—to the historic places, the beautiful parks, and the monuments. In Oslo, people walked everywhere. Bicycles and baby buggies filled the walkways. Laughing children in bright wool hand-knit sweaters and caps were like a painting in perpetual motion. Sedate dogs walked beside their owners. The weather was like a New England autumn. Bands played in the parks. Guitars were strummed on the streets.

The most memorable monument was the Resistance Building, the historical museum that honored the bravery of the Norwegian Freedom Fighters and the people of Norway during the Nazi occupation. Monuments of Franklin D. Roosevelt and Winston Churchill were at the entrance. "Never Again" was the theme. I was proud to be an American and proud to be a part of these Norwegian people.

The churches were beautiful but empty. Too many Europeans felt indifferent to their spiritual needs. Their fear of nuclear war was greater than their fear of eternity without God.

Bjorne and Rut took us to the Philadelphia Church in Oslo, where we heard the Swedish chorus from Stockholm. What music! The young people from the Philadelphia Church go out, with their guitars, into the streets to witness to others about God's love. One Saturday night sixteen-hundred young people gathered at the church to sing and praise the Lord. That night many young people threw off the shackles of sin to walk in God's grace and newness of life. *That was Papa's kind of meeting!*

From the Langmo home we made contact with our Norwegian relatives. Once again we were on a train, this time to Porsgruno where my cousin Sigrid, the daughter of one of Papa's sisters, and her husband, Rolf, a stocky, earthy man with gray-blond hair and blue eyes, spoke English. His delightful humor kept us laughing most of the time.

When we arrived at their lovely home, Sigrid proved the gracious hostess, setting a picturesque table with steaming coffee and delicious apple cake. We sat around the table laughing and reminiscing as they recalled my father's visit so many years ago. Later, we met their beautiful children and their brave, young grandson who suffered massive burns in a tragic accident. His determination to live helped make medical history.

Rolf and Sigrid arranged a reunion with other cousins and we enjoyed our first delicious elk roast dinner.

When we met these cousins and their families—one of them by going up a winding mountain road—we could see family resemblances. I marveled at the grace of God that kept these Norwegian people in His loving care. They, too, had come through many dangers, toils, and snares.

Memories of the Nazi occupation remain deep in their hearts—the years they were forced out of their homes and watched the enemy build bunkers in their lovely gardens. Their food was taken. Their men were captured and many were shot on the spot. Still they resisted!! Here and there in Norway there is still evidence of the bunkers—rusty, iron barricades and wired fences left behind by the retreating Germans. They have these memories, but they also have memories of their bravery as they resisted the enemy.

Above all, I found my relatives to be a proud, stoic people—beautiful women, strong men, with lovely homes and gracious hospitality. Their homes shone with a scrubbed cleanliness. No wonder Mama had starched curtains—even in the outhouse—and always seemed to have a beautiful sense of order. In Norway, handmade rugs, original paintings, and handcrafts of various kinds graced each home.

The women were constantly hand-knitting beautiful sweaters. Even young children learned to knit.

Yes, these were my people. These were my roots. I felt a special pride in the stone fences, the gardens, and the brilliant foliage of fall that reminded me of New England. The people of Norway treasure beauty—beauty in art, music, and the "hidden art" that Edith Schaeffer mentions: a table, special china, a meal. Every table setting was a work of art—a change of beautiful china cups; the arrangement of assorted cheeses, meat and fish; and decoration with cucumbers, tomatoes, or green pepper slices. There was even originality in the delicately folded napkins—fluffed like a flower in the empty coffee cups.

The natural resources of the country were displayed in these homes—colorful tile, marble, glass, and beautiful grains of wood. The art of hand-embroidered tablecloths, rugs, and pillows showed not only the creativity, but the dignity of labor. I had read once that "the beauty of life is godliness. The beauty of a home is order." There in Norway, as well as in my travels through America, I could "feel" a Scandinavian home and sense the beauty of cleanliness.

Creativity was all around me. But God's creation was in the hearts of those we met. While Rolf was picking raspberries one morning, a girl asked, "Isn't that a lot of work?"

"Work?" Rolf responded. "Oh, no, a blessing from God."

On Saturday it seemed that everyone was outside, walking, jogging, bicycling, or strolling with baby buggies and well-trained dogs. The stores were crowded at all times; yet, we always managed to find a corner for a coffee break.

The "walking street," famous porcelain and glass factories, beautiful stores where clerks speak English and offer helpful service—each beautiful scene was tucked away in our chest of memories.

Yet it is the people we keep in our hearts—Papa's family! Throughout his lifetime, Papa instilled in me his love of books, his love of words, his love of God, his love of people, and his love of Norway. From the moment Harold and Janice and I reached the European continent, all the Scandinavian people, the museums, the monuments, the music, the countryside were merely steppingstones to Papa's place—a journey that would help me know him better.

But before we went on to Papa's place—to the place where he was born and lived as a child—we would take a journey to Lista, Norway—Mama's birthplace and the town where Mama's family still lives.

[illegible] we went on to Papa's place—to the place where he was born and lived as a child—we would take a journey [illegible] and the town [illegible]

19

Lista

In the early morning Sigrid packed a lunch before Rolf took us on a three-hour drive to Lista in the southern part of Norway.

We stopped at places of historical interest like the Ibsen Memorial, the famous Terje Vigen Monument and grave. Through the years, Mama's rendition of Henrik Ibsen's immortal poem had made the hero, Terje Vigen, real to us. We also saw the memorial to famous pirates. This was the one that would intrigue the grandchildren when we got back to North Carolina. It would be the pirate-heroes they would want to claim as relatives.

Jan found a quaint village bakery with a coffee shop upstairs. With his sense of humor, Rolf quipped, "I always knew it was there—just didn't know where they put it."

When we forgot something, Rolf chuckled, "Somebody needs a new roof." Rolf's humor was surface and light-hearted, but his thoughtfulness and giving of time were deep. They came from a man who had lived with life and death and faced war as a pilot—but a man who still viewed life from a positive perspective.

Along the way to Lista, we found a spot overlooking one of the many fjords, and we enjoyed the lunch Sigrid had prepared, not forgetting the coffee. It was a leisurely journey with all the beauty of Norway's mountains, fjords, waterfalls, valleys, and the great North Sea to enjoy.

We arrived in the city of Farsund built so long ago by the Lunds. Husan, the famous Lund residence of a bygone era, overlooked the harbor. It, too, was once occupied by the Nazi forces. Later it became the City Hall, where banquets and receptions are still held.

After touring Farsund, we drove to nearby Lista, where many Farsund residents have summer homes. Lista's famous lighthouse looks out over the harbor where the North Sea stretches to England. Strong winds and mist from the sea kept us bundled in coats and scarves while we watched the waves roll over the shore of Lista. This is where my mother played as a child. The open fields, homes, and barns formed a picturesque, peaceful valley. Only a few ugly Nazi bunkers left their grim reminder of war.

The North Sea, ever-changing, had rolled on through war and peace. The people—these sturdy, strong-willed Norwegians—had lived through their joys and tears, planted their gardens again and rebeautified their homes. Once again lace curtains and window boxes looked out over the flowers, and the lighthouse kept watch over the sea as mist and wind continued to blow over the shoreline.

At four in the afternoon we arrived at the summer home of Dr. Sverre Reinertsen. We had never met before this time.

A friend from Brooklyn, New York, had sent *First We Have Coffee* to Dr. Reinertsen, a surgeon in Stavanger, Norway. When the doctor read the book, he realized we were related, and sent a letter written in perfect English to me.

When he heard about our pending trip to Europe, he graciously made plans for a family reunion at his home.

The newlyfound relatives welcomed us to the family. Within a short time, others arrived and the house was filled with joyous greetings. As our gracious hostess, Nellie Reinertsen, served her homemade coffee cakes and whipped-cream cakes, we shared our stories and memories. Jan was asked to give a rendition of Mama's favorite poem, "The Touch of the Master's Hand." Jan summed it up with a personal testimony about God's love for us. "When God tunes our lives," she said, "we make beautiful music."

Looking over these people who were a part of me, I knew God was tuning up an orchestra.

On Sunday, a gray, misty day, we joined other relatives, the Nordhassels as well as the Reinertsens, at the Vanse Kirk. It was raining when we went to church, but a quiet hush fell over us as we entered the 950-year-old historic Lutheran church.

Generations had worshiped here. Their children had been baptized and confirmed here. And this was where Mama attended church until she was fifteen and left for America. For a few moments I pictured Mama as the four-year-old child, Elvina, and her five-year-old brother, Joe, sitting side by side with a relative in this old church. They were too young to understand why their mother had left for America. They only remembered her sobbing as she walked away. I could almost hear Joe say, "Elvina, we must be very good, and someday we'll go to our mother." When Joe was fifteen he left for America. One year later, Mama followed.

Now Janice, Harold, and I sat beside the Reinertsens and the Nordhassels as the organ music broke the silence. Candles flickered. A young Lutheran priest in ornate robes stood in the high pulpit and opened the Bible.

I listened carefully and was able to understand my childhood language. What I didn't understand with my mind, I understood with my heart. This young Lutheran priest was speaking in the power of the Holy Spirit. His message was clear—the greatest need in the world was not food alone, but the Bread of Life, Jesus Christ as Savior and Lord. We were one in spirit with a desire to see a spiritual awakening not only in Norway, but throughout the world.

After his message, we quietly followed our family to the altar where we knelt together for communion. Kneeling there, I thought of Mama. Mama had given me a good beginning. Like she had always said, "There was room at the cross for all generations past and all generations to come."

We stood for the benediction, then we silently left the church.

Even in the misty rain, there was peace as we walked through the old graveyard and saw the names of generations past. I remembered again, "Lord, thou hast been our dwelling place in all generations" (Psalm 90:1).

Seated around the Sunday dinner table, we once again enjoyed the gracious Nordhassel hospitality, their lovely daughters Liv and Asta, and the red-gold-haired granddaughter, the family's "Golden Girl."

All that day family history and stories were interwoven with the present, a blending of joy and sorrow.

Jan said, "We wanted to forget the past with its grief, but God wanted us to redeem it."

Out of the "all things"—God had worked!

We remembered the past and its sorrows with love and understanding. God had blessed many through Bertilda and Jergen Johannasen's children: Mama and Uncle Joe. In meeting Mama's family in Lista, even some she never knew, I could see the same creative love and kindness in them that was so much a part of Mama and Uncle Joe. I was proud of my heritage.

And I was proud to meet the family of the grandfather I never knew. When I walk the sandy shore of North Carolina, I will think of him as he sailed the seas. I will recall his last lonely years walking the shores of Lista, Norway.

God has His own way of bringing blessing out of life's "all things." One day we will all meet in heaven and sing the story, "Saved by grace."

Once again—there in the land of no tears—Mama, Papa, and I will sing, "Great is Thy faithfulness, Lord, unto me!"

20

Papa's Homeplace

From Porsgruno, Rolf drove over winding roads, through valleys and hills until we saw a sign marked Bamble. Then, turning around the rocky bends, we saw where the road led to a mailbox: Tveten. My heart skipped a beat.

Following the lane from the mailbox we saw the white, sturdy house on the right, the barns on the left. "So this is Papa's homeplace!" I exclaimed as we walked to the house where Elius N. Tveten, one of nine children, was born on May 18, 1888.

No curtains hung in the windows. No flower boxes looked out on the overgrown gardens. The sounds of living had echoed into the past.

Harold and Rolf walked around the barns while Jan and I followed a rocky trail to Papa's potato field. Nestled in the hills was a valley of rich soil where Papa had planted his gardens. Long ago, during one of Papa's rare sentimental moods, he had told me about walking hand in hand with his mother to the potato field. In the middle of planting, she had stopped and said, "Look up, Elius, and listen to the song of the potato bird." Hand in hand again, mother and son stood to listen.

I knew how Papa felt. My grandchildren enjoy working with me in the garden. In the middle of work someone will say, "Look at that butterfly," or, "Watch the squirrels," and we stop to look. Then it's back to work and the children drop cut potatoes into the holes. Kathryn decides it is faster to dump a bucketful into a hole and our dog Yenta, a yellow Lab, retrieves the hidden potatoes. We face a challenge—but the result will be potatoes for the whole neighborhood.

I could visualize my grandmother, Papa's mother, doing what I enjoy doing—walking to the garden with a child's hand in one hand, a hoe in the other.

As I stood at Papa's place looking over the valley, I saw a rocky hill like a huge boulder. That had to be the place my father had wistfully described. To him it probably had a greater significance than we could know. But the fact that he mentioned a specific place gave it special meaning to me. Standing there, Janice and I shared our thoughts about the places we had seen: the one-room, framed schoolhouse that remained unchanged; the Lutheran church with the steeple, where the Twetens were baptized, confirmed, married, and buried; the graveyard with its *Tveten* gravemarkers and memorials to past generations. We talked about the four farms where my father worked while attending school and the four-mile, rocky, dusty road to the schoolhouse.

In my mind I heard, *You can't go home again.* But in my heart I knew *we can go home again.* I did! I came "home" to the roots where part of me belongs. I came "home" to learn a deeper understanding of how to bring the past into the present. In knowing the past, I can prepare better for the future.

The wind blew through the trees surrounding Papa's lonely childhood home. The barn was silent. The cows, chickens, and horses were gone. The overgrown gardens were a reminder of another time when fruit trees blossomed in the spring, flowers grew in window boxes and the house rang with the sounds of living.

Now the wind sighed over the lonely valley as the sun fingered over the "rock" near the potato field. Reluctantly, we turned to leave. I took one final glance back over a time that is no more.

I settled back in Rolf's car and tried to imagine what life had been. Stories from the past come slowly for the Norwegian people. They carry their sorrows inside and move into the living present with patience and courage.

I was hearing stories that my father never told. Therefore, I knew the "rock" that he had mentioned had to be special to him.

Putting the bits and pieces together in my heart, I found my thoughts going back to a long-ago time, a time that could have been. I saw a young, golden-haired, blue-eyed boy running across the open field, thin coat open, hair blowing in the wind, to climb up on his "rock." With arms outstretched he shouted to the world, "I'm king of the mountain!"

This was Papa's place as a young child.

I visualized him walking slowly beside his mother later as they followed a small coffin to the graveyard. One of his sisters, his playmate, died from the Black Sickness, a type of influenza. Papa watched the family nail a black cross on the door. Not understanding any of it, the young boy, Elius, ran to his place, to the rock. There he sobbed alone.

When spring came, the gentle mother took Elius by the hand. "Come, we plant potatoes." Living goes on.

Another day came when another black cross was nailed on the door, then another, and another, until the young Elius had seen four crosses, one after the other, nailed to the door of his home. The wind howled over the churchyard. Elius ran to his rock again and again and cried alone. Perhaps he wondered if he would be next to go in a box.

Then spring came, as it always does, even after the winter of the soul, and there was the cry of a newborn baby. Then a year later, there was another sound of new life.

Knute, the eldest son, helped his father till the soil and cut the timber. For Elius there was not time for play since his fragile mother needed his help to plant the garden, do the chores, and care for the little ones.

Then there came another time when from the top of his "rock" he heard the sound of death—hammers nailing another black cross on the door. This time, the strong father had died. The mother, a new life within her, held the young girls while eight-year-old Elius and Knute, fourteen, watched in utter despair.

Knute tilled the land, cut the timber, and Elius tended to chores and gardens and watched over his frail mother. Once again the black day of sorrow came when the five surviving children stood around the grave of their mother. Knute was fifteen, Elius, nine, and the youngest of three little sisters was six months old.

Elius and the three sisters were taken into separate homes, where they remained for several years. Elius was boarded out to four different farmhomes, where he had chores to complete before and after school. When he was fifteen he returned to live with Knute until he went to America two years later.

Knute, too old for his years, stayed on the farm to till the land and cut timber. He stayed until he died at the age of ninety. He had gone to the woods with his lunch pail and ax. They found him there—sitting on a log—at rest from his labors.

Years later, Papa told me how terrified he was of the dark woods around his temporary home after his mother's death. He had to carry two pails of water from the spring through the woods and couldn't run. The sounds were magnified by fear of imaginary animals and the unbearable loneliness of being separated from his family.

Papa seldom spoke of his childhood, but when he returned from his trip to Norway to visit his homeplace after forty years, he told me about the "rock" and the song of the potato bird.

"I was so lonely in those strange homes, but when I could get away, I ran for miles to go up on the rock. Then I would call out over the valley, 'Mor, Mor' [Mother, Mother], but the echo returned." I can still hear Papa saying, "I longed for the time when we planted potatoes and listened to the song of the bird. I went back to that spot when I visited Norway and looked out over the valley. Margaret, for a moment the old grief returned," he admitted. "But suddenly, from out of the sky came the song of a bird. It seemed that the bird sang just for me. Then suddenly, it disappeared into the blue sky."

Is this when his anger built? I wondered. *Back then in his lonely childhood?*

I wanted Papa to tell me more about his childhood but he shrugged his shoulders. "Ja, ja, life is a mystery," he mused. Then quietly he returned to his books.

I leaned back against the seat of Rolf's car. For days now I had traced the roots of my beginnings. But had I not also traced the roots of Papa's anger? A boy orphaned early and tossed to and fro in foster homes, a boy too old for his years. Had the anger built in his soul as each family member died, as each black cross had been nailed to the door of his childhood? I thought of Papa and his fear of the dark woods after the death of his young mother. No wonder he had learned to escape into books. No wonder he didn't go on to the university to study more, to teach. His early years had been years of responsibility. He wasn't accustomed to following his dreams, only his chores.

But even in his childhood Papa had a rock to run to—it had set a pattern for his life. No wonder it was so easy for Papa to run to the Rock of Ages.

Before we realized it, Rolf was turning into the driveway of cousin Ella's lovely home. Inside, rustic walls held the trophies of her husband's hunting trips, and the aroma of coffee already filled the room.

Beautiful handiwork and her gourmet cooking showed Ella's creativity. Around the table we enjoyed the delicious food and the love and warmth of family and friends. We shared our faith in God, and when I sang an old Norwegian song, Himmel og jorg kan brenner, Ella reached for her guitar. We sat together singing, Ella strumming the guitar. It was a song about everything disappearing—the heavens and the earth, cliffs and valleys—but the one who believes God will know that His promises never change.

When the song ended, Ella gently handed me the guitar. "This was your father's guitar," she said softly. "When he went to America, he gave it to my mother. Before she died, she gave it to me. Now, Margaret, I give it to you."

Her beautiful expression stays before me even now. I can still see her clearly as she took my hands and said in Norwegian, "You pray for me, and I will pray for you."

You can go "home" again. Back to your roots, your heritage, your beginnings.

I did!

Gently, I close the lid on the treasure chest of the past. We have traveled far together—you and I—from the tent on the Canadian prairies back to the homeplace.

Now it is time to move together toward the tomorrows that are in God's hands—just as the yesterdays, with their winds and storms, sunshine and peace, were in God's faithful hands.

From the past we learn that God is faithful, and the faith of yesterday rekindles faith for today. We can trust Him with the depths of our sorrows for He is acquainted with grief.

We also learn that God even trusts us, with all our frailties, to be the bearers of His love.

God's covenant and our obedience will move into the tomorrows—from generation to generation. My heart is full of praise.

Somehow, throughout the courts of heaven I hear the sound of "Amazing Grace." Papa is in his place!

Papa, do you see this other young man? Across the miles from glory, can you see him so like you, Papa? Blond hair blown by the wind. Clear blue eyes. Strong and sturdy—a true Norwegian. Do you see him, Papa, as he looks out over his congregation? Do you see him step behind the sacred desk?

From the open Bible, do you hear the sound of "Amazing Grace"—"For God so loved the world"?

Do you see him now, Papa—this young preacher behind the pulpit—one so like yourself? The Reverend Mr. Robert Keiter. He's your grandson, Papa. He followed in your steps.

He too is in his place!

Epilogue: Personal Notes

C.H. Spurgeon once said, "Faith must make use of experiences and read them over to God, out of the register of sanctified memory, as a recorder to Him who cannot forget."

In my travels, many listeners have asked me about my living sisters.

Papa's Place has been a difficult book to write since I can share from only my perspective. Each one of my sisters could write their own story. But the more I went into the past, the more convinced I became that each one has to make a decision of the will—alone. Regardless of the storms of life, each one comes through the storm when the heart is set to live for God. We are not destroyed by the storm, but we are destroyed by unforgiveness.

Just as Papa ran to his rock in childhood, until he ran to the Rock of Ages, so each of us has to learn to stand on the sure foundation—the Solid Rock. Then the storms can come, but we still stand.

• • •

My sister Grace, who lived in Greensboro, North Carolina, the one "God exchanged for Bernice," came through the storms still standing on the Rock. Her talents and abilities have taken her to many places, but her heart was always "home" with her sisters and their families. Grace went Home in 1997, surrounded by her sisters singing the old songs of the faith.

Doris, the independent one, who always wanted to run away with Uncle Barney, came through her storms with her heart set and her feet and hands moving in obedience to the Lord. Doris and her husband, Dave Hammer, live up on the hill keeping watch over the valley of Stoneville, North Carolina. Their beacon light shows the way as their children, Doreen, Don, Davidson, and Duane, wend their way through their own storms toward home. There they come, with their families, to the rock on the hill.

Joyce Solveig, Papa's songbird, lives in Russelville, Arkansas, with her husband, Howard Jensen (Harold's brother). Together, they open their home to strangers and lonely ones. She keeps that "Scandinavian feel" in her creative touch, and many couples have come to the Rock of Ages through this home.

With Howard, she has that "safe and loved" place. Their children, Judy, Paul, and Steve, come with their families to rejoice in the Living Word.

Alice, Gordon's love, came through her storms of loneliness without her husband (our brother). She reaches out with compassion and understanding to the wounded people around her. In 1995 Alice slipped quietly Home in her sleep—to join Gordon. Gordon and Alice's children, Ray, Nancy, Don, and Kurt, come with their families to the place of safety, the Rock of Ages.

The youngest Tweten, Jeanelle, the one we called "Baby" in our growing-up days, lives in Wilmington, North Carolina, with her husband, Reverend Peter Stam.There probably has never been a child more loved, not only by her parents, but also by her sisters and brother. To Papa, she was his shining star, the one he could laugh and talk with. Together they went to Carnegie Hall for music lessons and recitals.

Papa stood in awe of Grace and her talents, but he stood amazed at his beautiful Jeanelle. During much illness as a baby, Papa carried Jeanelle on his shoulder and preached his sermons. Yet Jeanelle remained unspoiled and loved—a special gift from God to our family. When the rest of us were gone from the home, it was Jeanelle who was still there.

Knowing how loved she was, I'm sure Jeanelle suffered more deeply when she saw Papa, the one she loved, lash out at the rest of us with undeserved anger. (Uncle Barney had always said "there was a part of Papa no one could reach.")

The one who was loved the most has somehow suffered the most through her own storms. For her alone, Papa spent an entire night in prayer when he watched her heart breaking. She came through as gold, the gold we all hold in our treasure chest of memory. Ah, but it is not the story of storms we tell; it is the song of the soul set free. Jeanelle, through many dangers, toils, and snares has come through standing on the Rock.

It was Jeanelle who spent the final moments with Papa when he was in the hospital for tests. It was at that time that the great Communicator revealed to Papa what love he had missed—though he hadn't missed God's love.

It was Papa who always said, "Jeanelle, you are beautiful."

She smilingly answered, "That's because I take after my father."

In that final visit, when Jeanelle turned to leave the hospital room, once again Papa said, "Ja, ja, Jeanelle, you are beautiful." She turned from the door to look at him. "That's because I take after my father" she repeated for one final time.

Then when Papa was alone in the room, away from the family he loved, God took him Home!

Later God spoke to Jeanelle's heart, "All My children are beautiful. They take after their Father."

Jeanelle's daughter, Charlene, is beautiful like her mother. Across the miles in Texas it is Jeanelle's son, Robert, who stands behind the pulpit, in his place. The children come with their families to the Rock.

Since I am the eldest Tweten and have walked in God's love for many years, I have seen Mama's children reach out to bless the world—each in a special God-given way. I have also observed others who grew up in homes with ideal settings, without the winds of anger, yet I often see shipwrecked lives. Why? Perhaps there was no covenant with God.

Mama and her covenant with God stood on the Rock. Papa stood on the Rock of God's truth, and when I tremble or falter, the Rock of Ages never trembles under me.

Jesus didn't tell His disciples that a storm was coming. He simply said, "We're going over to the other side." Storms come: storms of anger, injustice, rejection, abuse, sickness or financial storms. They come! Without the Rock, Christ Jesus, we falter in quicksand. Grounded on the Rock, we can stand through the storms and come through on the other side.

Mama and Papa's children did! So will you and your children's children—if "on Christ the solid Rock" you stand, for "all other ground is sinking sand."

Heavenly Father,

Thank You for Your unconditional love for all of us, Mama and Papa's children. From my heart I thank You for my sisters, for their love for me and love for each other.

Together, we thank You, Father, for Your gift of amazing grace.

We love You, Lord. And we rejoice, Lord, that somewhere in the courts of heaven, Bernice and Gordon join Mama and Papa in the song of a soul set free. We know—because our hearts are singing with them.

To God be the glory!

Other Books by Margaret Jensen

All God's Children Got Robes

Filled with poignant and often humorous stories, Margaret relates her personal experience with cancer to powerfully illustrate God's faithfulness and provision. With her special gift of sharing and warm sense of humor, *All God's Children Got Robes* will encourage you in your faith.

First We Have Coffee

Margaret's warm stories of life as the daughter of a Scandinavian pastor in the Canadian north will touch your heart with timeless lessons of unwavering faith and family love. Margaret's mother is an indomitable character whose stern Norwegian discipline is matched only by her laughter and singing. The down-to-earth wisdom she passes on to both young and old over steaming cups of coffee will bring encouragement and hope to anyone who has gone through difficult times.

Lena

Margaret shares how she found a deeper relationship with God than she could have imagined through the exuberant, unshakable faith of a woman named Lena. Lena's strong, simple faith—her stories, songs, and laughter—will capture your heart and help you praise God until the joy comes.

A Nail in a Sure Place

Drawing on vibrant, real-life experiences, Margaret paints a colorful picture of God's sovereignty and provision. *A Nail in a Sure Place* will refresh your spirit and help you realize the power of God's love and faithfulness. These lively stories are perfect for encouraging your friends and for sharing the security and hope found in Jesus.

A View from the Top

With the wisdom garnered from a lifetime of experiences, Margaret looks back on events in her life and the lessons learned along the way. Written as a memoir to her grandchildren, Jensen's humorous and touching stories warm the heart and inspire the soul with tales of God's comfort in times of need. As you turn the pages and traverse the miles, you will learn about prayer, grace faithfulness, and walking in the power of God.

Other Good Harvest House Reading

A Place Called Simplicity
by *Claire Cloninger*

A warm invitation to freedom from a cluttered life and a breath of fresh air for everyone who longs to slow down and find balance in all areas of life.

Goodbye Is not Forever
by *Amy George* with *Al Janssen*

Amy was a baby when the Soviet secret police condemned her father to Siberia During World War II she witnessed firsthand the horrors of Hitler's Germany, yet also saw evidence that God's grace was at work long before she knew Him.

Healing the Hurting Heart
by *June Hunt*

With a compassionate heart, June Hunt responds to letters from hurting people with sound counsel and scriptural insights. Each short, to-the-point chapter gives heartfelt encouragement, straight talk, and "how to" steps to begin the journey to victory.

A Father for All Seasons
by *Bob Welch*

Bob Welch takes a joyful and contemplative look at the life-long love between fathers and sons. Welch reflects upon his own experiences and shares the everyday journeys of others in this collection of stories that is rich with humorous anecdotes, poignant lessons, and spiritual truths.